# SMART ROUTE TO THE TOEIC® L&R TEST

**Hiromi Furusawa**
**Braven Smillie**

NATIONAL GEOGRAPHIC
LEARNING

Australia • Brazil • Mexico • Singapore • United Kingdom • United States

NATIONAL GEOGRAPHIC LEARNING

**SMART ROUTE TO THE TOEIC® L&R TEST**

**Hiromi Furusawa / Braven Smillie**



**Photo Credits:**
Cover: © Surasak | Dreamstime.com; 11: © stock.adobe.com, © stock.adobe.com, © getty images; 27: © stock.adobe.com, © stock.adobe.com, © Yosef Yahav | Dreamstime.com; 35: © stock.adobe.com; 43: © stock.adobe.com; 89: © stock.adobe.com

For permission to use material from this textbook or product, e-mail to **elt@cengagejapan.com**

ISBN: 978-4-86312-395-3

**National Geographic Learning | Cengage Learning K.K.**
No. 2 Funato Building 5th Floor
1-11-11 Kudankita, Chiyoda-ku
Tokyo 102-0073
Japan

Tel: 03-3511-4392
Fax: 03-3511-4391

# はしがき

本書はTOEIC L&Rテストの対策を始めたばかりの方に向けたテキストです。スコアアップだけではなく、英語への関心を高め、一歩ずつ確実に英語力を伸ばすことができるよう、様々な工夫を盛り込んでいます。

**語彙への興味を高める工夫**

各Unitの冒頭で紹介するのは、テーマ毎のTOEIC頻出語句（20語前後）ですが、この中には必ず「カタカナ語」が含まれています。日常で使用される英語由来の言葉を取り上げ、正しい発音や意味を紹介しています（例:「エプロン」の正しい発音、「デパート≠ department = 部門、部署」）。これらに触れることで、英語に対する興味や学習意欲の向上が期待できます。更に、ここで紹介する語句は、同じUnit内の様々な問題に登場します。その中で自然に反復学習をしながら、語句の実際の用法を確認することができます。

**問題を解く前・後のトレーニング**

必要な英語力が身についていない段階でやみくもにTOEIC形式の問題を解いても、正解できる可能性は低く、学習意欲低下の大きな原因となります。これを避けるために、本書は、TOEIC形式の問題数はあえて少なくして、代わりに様々なトレーニング課題を用意しています。リスニングではディクテーション、リーディングでは単語の品詞や意味を調べたり、文書の一部を和訳したりする課題があり、それらに取り組んでいるうちに、「選ぶ理由がきちんとわかって正解できる問題数」が自然と増えるよう工夫しています。

**取り組みやすいPartからスタート**

本書の全体構成も独特です。TOEIC L&Rテストには Part 1～7がありますが、序盤のUnitでは、まずは取り組みやすいパート（Part 1, 2, 5, 7）に絞って学習を始め、中盤から徐々に他のパート（Part 3, 4, 6）へと範囲を広げていきます。このような構成にしたのは、難度の高いPartに最初から取り組むことが学習意欲の低下につながりかねないことを考慮したためです。本書では、適切な段階を経ながら、全てのパート対策が無理なく学習できるようになっています。

**正解するべき問題だけにフォーカス**

TOEIC L&Rテストは英検のようにレベル別に分かれた試験ではありません。難度が異なる問題がランダムに出題され、難度が高い問題だからといって高配点というわけでもありません。つまり、まんべんなく正解しようとするのではなく、まずは難度の低い問題から確実に正解できるようにすることが重要です。本書は、TOEIC L&Rテストに出る問題の中から入門者～初級者が「確実に正解するべき問題」だけに絞った1冊です。

本書がTOEIC L&Rテストのスコアだけではなく、英語への関心を高め、英語力そのものの向上の一助となることができればうれしく思います。

著者を代表して

古澤　弘美

# Table of Contents

| Part 3 | Part 4 | Part 5 | Part 6 | Part 7 |
|---|---|---|---|---|
| | | 品詞問題①名詞 ▶p.13 | | 読解問題全般 ▶p.15 |
| | | 品詞問題②形容詞 ▶p.21 | | 社内掲示物 ▶p.23 |
| | | 品詞問題③副詞 ▶p.29 | | リストを含む掲示物 ▶p.31 |
| | | 動詞①述語動詞の基本 ▶p.37 | | Eメール ▶p.39 |
| | | 動詞②態 ▶p.45 | | 一斉送信メール・通知 ▶p.47 |
| 長文リスニング問題の基本① ▶p.52 | | 動詞③数 ▶p.55 | | フォーム・定型用紙 ▶p.57 |
| | 長文リスニング問題の基本② ▶p.62 | 代名詞 ▶p.65 | | 広告文 ▶p.67 |
| 場面が社内の場合 ▶p.71 | 場面が社内の場合 ▶p.71 | 関係代名詞 ▶p.74 | | チャット・テキストメッセージ ▶p.76 |
| 電話の聞き取り ▶p.80 | 電話の聞き取り ▶p.80 | 前置詞 vs 接続詞① ▶p.83 | | 電話に関する文書 ▶p.85 |
| 言い換えへの対応 ▶p.90 | | 前置詞 vs 接続詞② ▶p.92 | | 請求書 ▶p.94 |
| | 人事に関するお知らせ ▶p.99 | | 文と文をつなぐ語句 ▶p.101 | 求人広告 ▶p.103 |
| グラフィック問題① ▶p.107 | グラフィック問題① ▶p.107 | 語句の組み合わせ① ▶p.111 | | レター ▶p.113 |
| | 少し複雑な設問 ▶p.118 | | 文脈依存型の問題 ▶p.120 | メディア関連の文書 ▶p.122 |
| 3名での会話 ▶p.127 | | 語句の組み合わせ② ▶p.129 | | NOT 問題 ▶p.131 |
| グラフィック問題② ▶p.135 | グラフィック問題② ▶p.135 | | 文挿入問題 ▶p.139 | ダブル・トリプルパッセージ ▶p.141 |

# 本書の構成と使い方

本書は、TOEIC L&R テストによく登場する場面やテーマごとに、全部で 15 Unit で構成されています。この 1 冊を通して、頻出項目の中でも「確実に押さえておきたいポイント」を段階的かつ網羅的に学ぶことができます。各 Unit は 8 ～ 10 ページで、次の 3 部に分かれています。

## 語彙紹介

各 Unit のテーマごとに厳選した重要語句の発音と意味をチェックします。このおよそ 20 の語句は、同じ Unit の中の問題文や選択肢などに登場しますので、その導入となっています。

TOEIC L&R 頻出のテーマ別に学びます。

Unit 1 Shopping

TOEIC では
この Unit では

Vocabulary Attack

1 カタカナ語になっている TOEIC 頻出語句を確認しましょう（音声リピートと意味をチェック）。

| | | | |
|---|---|---|---|
| store | 店、蓄える、保管する | cart | カート、手押し車 |
| apron | エプロン | item | 品物、商品 |
| counter | カウンター、台 | tray | トレー、盆 |
| bag | 袋、かばん | label | ラベル、札 |

2 その他の TOEIC 頻出語句をマスターしましょう。

❶ まずは音声を聞いてリピートしましょう。

| | | | |
|---|---|---|---|
| display | grocery | clerk | cashier |
| arrange | purchase | shopper | reach into |
| shelf | discount | grand opening | hardware |
| sign | in a row | hang | browse |

❷ 上の表の中から、下線部に適切な英語を選び入れましょう。

モノ
人
動作
その他

10

親しみやすいカタカナ語から学習スタート。

## リスニング学習

**攻略ポイント**の確認➡**段階的練習**➡ TOEIC 形式の問題に挑戦、という流れです。

本書の前半は Part 1 と 2 に絞って、短文のリスニング練習を行います。

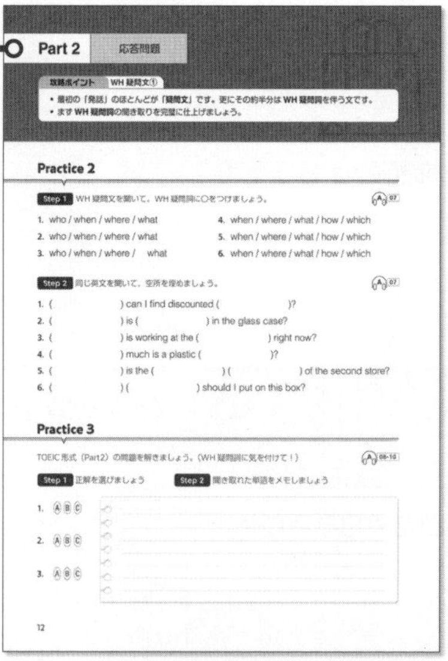
Part 2 応答問題

攻略ポイント WH 疑問文①

Practice 2

Step 1 WH 疑問文を聞いて、WH 疑問詞に○をつけましょう。

1. who / when / where / what
2. who / when / where / what
3. who / when / where / what
4. when / where / what / how / which
5. when / where / what / how / which
6. when / where / what / how / which

Step 2 同じ英文を聞いて、空所を埋めましょう。

1. ( ) can I find discounted ( )?
2. ( ) is ( ) in the glass case?
3. ( ) is working at the ( ) right now?
4. ( ) much is a plastic ( )?
5. ( ) is the ( ) ( ) of the second store?
6. ( ) ( ) should I put on this box?

Practice 3

Step 1 正解を選びましょう
Step 2 聞き取れた単語をメモしましょう

1. Ⓐ Ⓑ Ⓒ
2. Ⓐ Ⓑ Ⓒ
3. Ⓐ Ⓑ Ⓒ

12

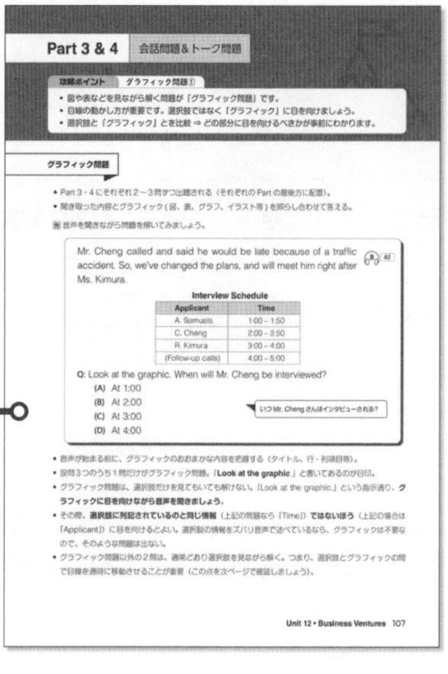
Part 3 & 4 会話問題＆トーク問題

攻略ポイント グラフィック問題①

グラフィック問題

Mr. Cheng called and said he would be late because of a traffic accident. So, we've changed the plans, and will meet him right after Ms. Kimura.

Interview Schedule

| Applicant | Time |
|---|---|
| A. Samuels | 1:00 – 1:50 |
| C. Cheng | 2:00 – 2:50 |
| R. Kimura | 3:00 – 4:00 |
| (Follow-up calls) | 4:00 – 5:00 |

Q: Look at the graphic. When will Mr. Cheng be interviewed?
(A) At 1:00
(B) At 2:00
(C) At 3:00
(D) At 4:00

Unit 12 • Business Ventures 107

中盤以降で Part 3 と 4 の対策を始め、徐々に難度を上げていきます。

## リーディング学習

リーディングは、文法・語彙・長文読解それぞれの**攻略ポイント**の確認➡**段階的練習**➡**TOEIC 形式の問題**に挑戦、という流れです。

Part 5 短文穴埋め問題

攻略ポイント 前置詞 vs 接続詞①

- 選択肢に前置詞と接続詞が並んでいたら、ここで学ぶ項目を意識して解きましょう。
- 前置詞と接続詞は、見た目では区別しにくいので、判別する方法をしっかり覚えましょう。

文法ポイント 前置詞・接続詞①

**前置詞**：名詞や動名詞（～ing）とセットで使う [前置詞＋名詞（句）・動名詞]
**接続詞**：節（S+V）と節を接着する [S+V 接続詞 S+V] [接続詞 S+V, S+V]

なぜ、この違いが重要？ ⇒ 同じような意味でも、用法が異なるから。

例 私は会議に遅れました、交通渋滞**のせいで**。
[接続詞] I was late for the meeting **because** traffic was heavy.
[前置詞] I was late for the meeting **because of** heavy traffic.

- TOEIC に頻出する前置詞＆接続詞①：例文を参考に、どちらの品詞か考えて○を付けましょう。

| 意味＆英単語 | | 品詞 | 例文 |
| --- | --- | --- | --- |
| 原因・理由（～だから、～が理由で） | because | 前・接 | S+V **because** it rained. |
| | because of | 前・接 | S+V **because of** rain. |
| | due to | 前・接 | S+V **due to** rain. |
| | since | 前・接 | S+V **since** it rained. |
| 譲歩（～だけれども・～にも関わらず） | despite | 前・接 | S+V **despite** rain. |
| | although | 前・接 | S+V **although** it rained. |
| | in spite of | 前・接 | S+V **in spite of** rain. |
| | while | 前・接 | S+V **while** it rained. |
| 条件（もし～なら） | if | 前・接 | S+V **if** it rains. |
| | in case of | 前・接 | S+V **in case of** rain |
| | in case that | 前・接 | S+V **in case that** it rains. |

覚え方のヒント
複数の単語がセットになっている場合があるので群前置詞・群接続詞を最後の単語で判断しよう。例 in spite **of** / due **to** / in case **that**

Unit 9 • Phone Calls 83

まずは、文法や語彙問題の重要ポイントをチェック。

穴埋めや和訳などの練習を経て TOEIC 形式の問題に挑戦。

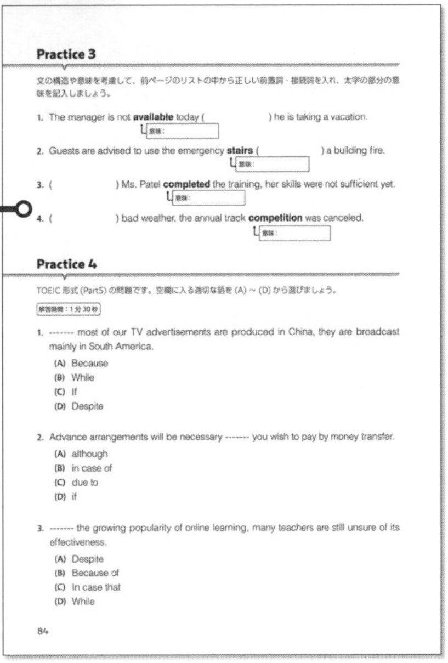
**Practice 3**

文の構造や意味を考慮して、前ページのリストの中から正しい前置詞・接続詞を入れ、太字の部分の意味を記入しましょう。

1. The manager is not **available** today ( ) he is taking a vacation.
   意味：
2. Guests are advised to use the emergency **stairs** ( ) a building fire.
   意味：
3. ( ) Ms. Patel **completed** the training, her skills were not sufficient yet.
   意味：
4. ( ) bad weather, the annual track **competition** was canceled.
   意味：

**Practice 4**

TOEIC 形式 (Part5) の問題です。空欄に入る適切な語を (A) ~ (D) から選びましょう。

解答時間：1分30秒

1. ------- most of our TV advertisements are produced in China, they are broadcast mainly in South America.
   (A) Because
   (B) While
   (C) If
   (D) Despite
2. Advance arrangements will be necessary ------- you wish to pay by money transfer.
   (A) although
   (B) in case of
   (C) due to
   (D) if
3. ------- the growing popularity of online learning, many teachers are still unsure of its effectiveness.
   (A) Despite
   (B) Because of
   (C) In case that
   (D) While

84

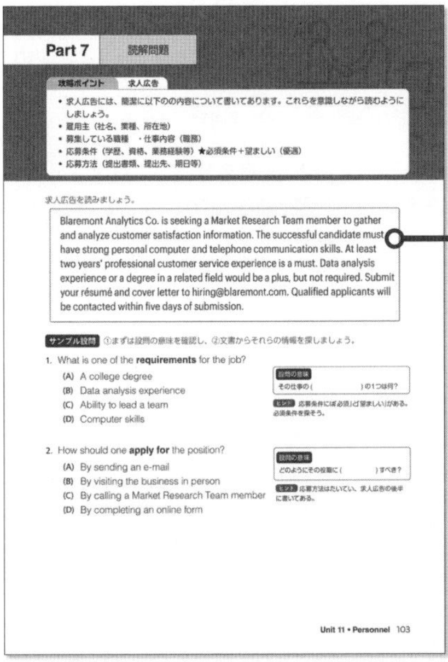
Part 7 読解問題

攻略ポイント 求人広告

- 求人広告には、簡潔に以下のの内容について書いてあります。これらを意識しながら読むようにしましょう。
- 雇用主（社名、業種、所在地）
- 募集している職種 ・仕事内容（職務）
- 応募条件（学歴、資格、業務経験等）★必須条件＋望ましい（優遇）
- 応募方法（提出書類、提出先、期日等）

求人広告を読みましょう。

Blaremont Analytics Co. is seeking a Market Research Team member to gather and analyze customer satisfaction information. The successful candidate must have strong personal computer and telephone communication skills. At least two years' professional customer service experience is a must. Data analysis experience or a degree in a related field would be a plus, but not required. Submit your résumé and cover letter to hiring@blaremont.com. Qualified applicants will be contacted within five days of submission.

サンプル設問 ①まずは設問の意味を確認し、②文書からそれらの情報を探しましょう。

1. What is one of the **requirements** for the job?
   (A) A college degree
   (B) Data analysis experience
   (C) Ability to lead a team
   (D) Computer skills

   設問の意味 その仕事の（ ）の1つは何？
   ヒント 応募条件には「必須」と「望ましい」がある。必須条件を探そう。

2. How should one **apply for** the position?
   (A) By sending an e-mail
   (B) By visiting the business in person
   (C) By calling a Market Research Team member
   (D) By completing an online form

   設問の意味 どのようにその役職に（ ）すべき？
   ヒント 応募方法はたいてい、求人広告の後半に書いてある。

Unit 11 • Personnel 103

長文読解では、文書別のポイントを学び、注目すべき点を確認してから問題に挑戦。

答え合わせの前には、重要な箇所の部分和訳にも取り組みます。

**精読タイム！** 1語1語に注目しながら、正確に和訳しましょう。

設問の精読
3. According to the ad, what **is required** for the job?
   この広告によると、その仕事には何が（ ）？
4. What should a **job seeker** do to make **an appointment**?
   （ ）は、（ ）をするために、何をするべき？

文書の精読 ★重要な部分だけ！

**Applicants** must be ready ① to work in the deli and **grocery** sections of our stores,
（ ）は～ができなくてはなりません。①総菜と（ ）売り場で働き、
and ② to accept **assignments** to different store locations.
②別店舗での（ ）も引き受けることが（できなくてはなりません）。

A high-school **diploma** is required
高校の（ ）は必須です。

To request an **interview** appointment, visit us online at www.lovecart-jobappl.com.
（ ）の予約を取るためには、www.lovecart-jobappl.com を訪問してください。

選択肢の精読 ★重要な部分だけ！

No. 3 (A) A food safety **certificate** 食品安全（ ）
(C) Working at **multiple** locations （ ）拠点での勤務
No. 4 (A) Call the **closest** store location （ ）店舗に電話する
(B) Mail a list of **references** to Houston
Houston に（ ）リストを郵送する

**Reflection**

Unit 11 で学んだ単語・表現をチェックしましょう。 意味がすぐに浮かぶようになるまで、反復練習しましょう。

| | | | |
| --- | --- | --- | --- |
| □ opening | □ position | □ résumé | □ career |
| □ seek | □ qualification | □ vacancy | □ candidate |
| □ degree | □ reference | □ apply for | □ benefits |
| □ paid vacation | □ submit | □ certificate | □ diploma |
| □ experience | □ temporary | □ hire | □ personnel |
| □ board member | □ promotion | □ retirement | □ moreover |
| □ therefore | □ however | □ additionally | □ instead |

Unit 11 • Personnel 105

最後は、Unit で学んだ重要語句のリスト。振り返りに役立てましょう。

# TOEIC Listening & Reading Test について

TOEIC とは Test of English for International Communication の略で、世界160ヵ国で実施されている英語コミュニケーション能力を評価するためのテストです。TOEICには数種類ありますが、より一般的なのは、リスニング＆リーディングに特化したテストです。本書はそのテスト対策のための教科書です。

TOEIC Listening & Reading Test はテスト結果が合格・不合格ではなく、リスニングセクション5点～495点、リーディングセクション5点～495点、トータル10点～990点のスコアで評価されます。

題材にはビジネスや一般的なコミュニケーションの場面が採用されています。特殊なビジネスの知識を必要としたり、特定の国や歴史、文化を知らなければ答えられない設問は含まれていません。

## 問題形式と内容

**リスニングセクション（約45～47分・100問）**

| | | | |
|---|---|---|---|
| **Part 1** | 写真描写問題 | 6問 | 1枚の写真について4つの短い説明文が1度だけ放送されます。説明文は印刷されていません。4つのうち写真を最も適切に描写しているものを選ぶ問題です。 |
| **Part 2** | 応答問題 | 25問 | 1つの質問または発言と、3つの応答がそれぞれ1度だけ放送されます。質問に対して最も適切な応答を選ぶ問題です。 |
| **Part 3** | 会話問題 | 39問 | 会話が1度だけ放送され、その後設問が続きます。会話は印刷されていません。問題用紙の設問と選択肢を読み、4つの選択肢の中から最も適切なものを選ぶ問題です。 |
| **Part 4** | 説明文問題<br>* 本書ではトーク問題 | 30問 | アナウンスやナレーションなどのトークが1度だけ放送され、その後設問が続きます。トークは印刷されていません。問題用紙の設問と選択肢を読み、4つの選択肢の中から最も適切なものを選ぶ問題です。 |

**リーディングセクション（約75分・100問）**

| | | | |
|---|---|---|---|
| **Part 5** | 短文穴埋め問題 | 30問 | 4つの選択肢の中から最も適切なものを選び、不完全な文を完成させる問題です。 |
| **Part 6** | 長文穴埋め問題 | 16問 | 4つの選択肢の中から最も適切なものを選び、不完全な文書を完成させる問題です。 |
| **Part 7** | 読解問題 | 1つの文書<br>29問<br>複数の文書<br>25問 | いろいろな内容・形式の、1つもしく複数の文書に関する問題が出題されます。設問を読み、4つの選択肢の中から最も適切なものを選ぶ問題です。 |

※リスニングセクションにおけるナレーションの発音は米国・英国・カナダ・オーストラリアです。

※本書では、初級者向けであることを考慮し、難度が比較的高い、以下の設問タイプの対策は含めておりません。
- Part 7 文挿入位置問題
- Part 7 トリプルパッセージ問題（ダブルパッセージ問題のみあり）

## 音声ファイルの利用方法

A 01 のアイコンがある箇所の音声ファイルにアクセスできます。

https://ngljapan.com/sr-toeic-audio/

❶ 上記の URL にアクセス、または QR コードをスマートフォンなどのリーダーでスキャン

❷ 表示されるファイル名をクリックして音声ファイルをダウンロードまたは再生

## 無料のオンライン学習ツール Quizlet でボキャビル！

https://quizlet.com/NGL_Japan/folders/smart-route-to-the-toeic-lr-test/sets

上記 URL にパソコンでアクセス、または QR コードをスマートフォンなどのリーダーでスキャンすると、各ユニット末の Reflection で取り上げている語句をクイズ形式で手軽に学習することができます。

# Unit 1 Shopping

**TOEIC では**
• 様々な「小売店」が題材として多数登場します。

**この Unit では**
• 小売店でよく登場する語句・会話表現・文書などに親しみましょう。
• 文法は「名詞」を深く学びましょう。

## Vocabulary Attack

**1** カタカナ語になっている TOEIC 頻出語句の音声を聞いてリピートし、意味を確認しましょう。 A 02

| | | | |
|---|---|---|---|
| store | 店、蓄える、保管する | cart | カート、手押し車 |
| apron | エプロン | item | 品物、商品 |
| counter | カウンター、台 | tray | トレー、盆 |
| bag | 袋、かばん | label | ラベル、札 |

**2** その他の TOEIC 頻出語句をマスターしましょう。

❶ まずは音声を聞いてリピートしましょう。 A 03

| | | | |
|---|---|---|---|
| display | grocery | clerk | cashier |
| arrange | purchase | shopper | reach into |
| shelf | discount | grand opening | hardware |
| sign | in a row | hang | browse |

❷ 上の表の中から、下線部に適切な英語を選び入れましょう。

**モノ**

貼り紙、看板、標識
→ ______________

食料品
→ ______________

棚
→ ______________

金物
→ ______________

**人**

買い物客
→ ______________

店員・事務員
→ ______________

レジ係
→ ______________

**動作**

～を購入する
→ ______________

並べて置く
→ ______________

掛ける、吊るす
→ ______________

～の中に手を伸ばす → ______________

～を閲覧する、ぶらぶら見て回る
→ ______________

**その他**

値引き（する）
→ ______________

開店イベント
→ ______________

陳列・展示（する）
→ ______________

並んで、一列で
→ ______________

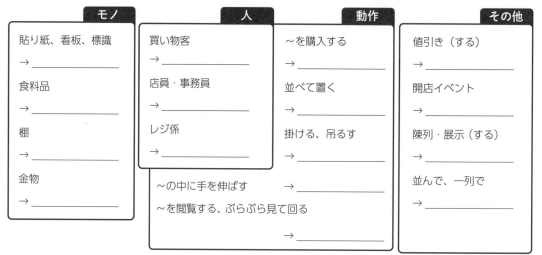

# Part 1 写真問題

**攻略ポイント** 写真問題の基本：動作に注目

- 音声を聞く前に写真を見て、英語で語句を思い浮かべましょう。
- 動詞に特に集中して聞き取りましょう。

## Practice 1

**事前に確認** どんな単語を使って写真を表現するか、各自またはペアで思い描きましょう。

例 I see モノ in this picture. / I think she(he) is ～ing. / I think she(he) is in the 場所.

**Step 1** 音声を聞き、写真を正しく描写している選択肢にマークしましょう。 A 04-06

**Step 2** 再び音声を聞き、空所を埋めてから、もう一度正解を選びましょう。 A 04-06

**1.**

**Step 1** Ⓐ Ⓑ

**Step 2**

(A) She is (                    ) a book.

(B) She is (                    ) a book.

**2.**

**Step 1** Ⓐ Ⓑ Ⓒ

**Step 2**

(A) He is (                    ) an apron.

(B) He is (                    ) an apron.

(C) He is (                    ) an apron.

**3.**

**Step 1** Ⓐ Ⓑ Ⓒ Ⓓ

**Step 2**

(A) The clerk is (                    ) to a (                    ).

(B) The clerk is (                    ) a (                    ).

(C) The clerk is (                    ) into a (                    ).

(D) The clerk is (                    ) a (                    ).

（注）本番のテストでは、問題冊子に英文は一切載っていません。全て音で聞いて判断できるよう、繰り返し練習しましょう。

# Part 2 応答問題

**攻略ポイント** WH 疑問文①

- 最初の「発話」のほとんどが**「疑問文」**です。更にその約半分は **WH 疑問詞**を伴う文です。
- まず **WH 疑問詞**の聞き取りを完璧に仕上げましょう。

## Practice 2

**Step 1** WH 疑問文を聞いて、WH 疑問詞に○をつけましょう。 07

1. who / when / where / what
2. who / when / where / what
3. who / when / where / what
4. when / where / what / how / which
5. when / where / what / how / which
6. when / where / what / how / which

**Step 2** 同じ英文を聞いて、空所を埋めましょう。 07

1. (　　　　　　　) can I find discounted (　　　　　　　)?
2. (　　　　　　　) is (　　　　　　　) in the glass case?
3. (　　　　　　　) is working at the (　　　　　　　) right now?
4. (　　　　　　　) much is a plastic (　　　　　　　)?
5. (　　　　　　　) is the (　　　　　　　) (　　　　　　　) of the second store?
6. (　　　　　　　) (　　　　　　　) should I put on this box?

## Practice 3

TOEIC 形式（Part 2）の問題を解きましょう。（WH 疑問詞に気を付けて！） 08-10

**Step 1** 正解を選びましょう。 **Step 2** 聞き取れた単語をメモしましょう。

1. Ⓐ Ⓑ Ⓒ
2. Ⓐ Ⓑ Ⓒ
3. Ⓐ Ⓑ Ⓒ

# Part 5 短文穴埋め問題

**攻略ポイント** 品詞問題①名詞

- 選択肢に、語尾が異なるだけの単語が並んでいたら「品詞問題」と考えましょう。
- 語尾から品詞が判断できるよう、しっかり練習しましょう。
- 空所の前後から「入れるべき品詞」を検討すると、素早く正確に解答できます。

**文法ポイント** 名詞

- 人・モノ・概念の名称を表す語　例 doctor, book, peace
- 冠詞（the / an）は名詞に付く　例 **a** teacher, **the** train
- 所有格（your / their / his など）は名詞に付く　例 **her** job, **its** office
- 前置詞＋名詞という形になる　例 **in** the room, **with** friends
- 主語や目的語になる　例 The store（主語（～は）） sells groceries（目的語（～を））.
- 主な名詞の語尾の特徴

| | |
|---|---|
| -er / or | play**er** / operat**or** |
| -ty | identi**ty** |
| -tion / -sion | ac**tion** / ses**sion** |
| -ness | happi**ness** |
| -nce / -nse | scie**nce** / offe**nse** |
| -ment | arrange**ment** |

（注：例外もあります。slow**er** 形容詞の比較級、swea**ty** 形容詞など）

## Practice 4

上記の「語尾の特徴」を参考に、次の A ～ D の語の中から**名詞**を選び、[　　] に ✓ をつけましょう。
※1行に1つずつとは限りません。

| | A | B | C | D |
|---|---|---|---|---|
| 1 | [　] real | [　] reality | [　] realize | [　] really |
| 2 | [　] differently | [　] different | [　] difference | [　] differ |
| 3 | [　] compete | [　] competitive | [　] competition | [　] competitor |
| 4 | [　] flat | [　] flatly | [　] flatten | [　] flatness |
| 5 | [　] measurement | [　] measurer | [　] measurable | [　] measurably |

## Practice 5

Practice 4 の単語から、以下の英文に合うものを選んで（　　）に記入しましょう。

1. Our online shop has received the second prize in the (　　　　　　　　).
   コンテスト

2. There are a lot of (　　　　　　　　) between these two products.
   違い（注：複数形で）

3. Many researchers predict that digital banks will soon become a (　　　　　　　　).
   現実

4. All (　　　　　　　　) must be double-checked before placing an order.
   寸法（注：複数形で）

## Practice 6

TOEIC 形式（Part 5）の問題です。空欄に入る適切な語を (A) ~ (D) から選びましょう。

解答時間：1 分 30 秒

1. The ------- of both our customers and employees is always our top priority.
   (A) safe
   (B) safely
   (C) save
   (D) safety

2. This executive suite is reserved for someone with a position of -------.
   (A) important
   (B) importance
   (C) importantly
   (D) imported

3. The management considers ABC Trading as their main -------.
   (A) compete
   (B) competitiveness
   (C) competitor
   (D) competitive

# Part 7 読解問題

**攻略ポイント** 読解問題全般

- 文書の内容を全て読み取ろうとしないことが重要です。問題を解く上で重要な部分だけを読み取りましょう。
- 設問・選択肢も英語で書かれています。この読み取りにも注意が必要です。
- 頻出する文書のパターンに慣れると、読みやすくなります。

店頭に掲示されるお知らせ（notice）を読みましょう。

> ## *Winslow's*
>
> Open 6:00 A.M. to 9:30 P.M. —weekdays
> 8:00 A.M. to 11:30 P.M. —weekends
>
> ◆ **Open 365 days a year**
> Whether you need organic meats, fresh-baked bread or delicious fruits and vegetables, Winslow's has them all—every day.
>
> ◆ **Join Winslow's Shopping Club**
> Get deep discounts on all items with club discount labels.
> *How do you join?* It's easy. Just ask your cashier, or fill out an application form at the customer service counter!

**サンプル設問** ①まずは設問の意味を確認し、②文書からそれらの情報を探しましょう。

1. **What time does** Winslow's **close** on Wednesday?
   (A) At 6:00 A.M.
   (B) At 8:00 A.M.
   (C) At 9:30 P.M.
   (D) At 11:30 P.M.

**設問の意味**
Winslow's は（　　　　　　　　）、水曜日には？

**ヒント** Wednesday の言い換えを文書から探そう。

2. What should a shopper do **to join** Winslow's Shopping Club?
   (A) Talk to a store clerk
   (B) Visit a store Web site
   (C) Buy discounted items
   (D) Pay a membership fee

**設問の意味**
買い物客は何をすべきですか？
Winslow's Shopping Club に（　　　　　　　　）？

**ヒント** Winslow's Shopping Club について書いている部分と、選択肢を見比べよう。

## Practice 7

読解問題に挑戦しましょう。

**解き方の手順**

1. まずは文書の種類を確認しましょう。 notice ⇒ お知らせ
2. 続いて設問を読んで「何を答えないといけないか」チェックしましょう。
3. 本文だけではなく文書の隅々にまで目を向けましょう。

この部分に書いてあります。

Questions 3-4 refer to the following notice.

解答時間：２分

# *Shay Hardware Outlet*

New Cranberry Mall Location

Grand Opening

**Saturday-Sunday, July 1-2**

**10 am – 8 pm**

Shay Hardware Outlet is opening a new store in the Cranberry Shopping Mall. Don't miss our Grand Opening celebration at the new store!

During the Grand Opening, ALL VISITORS can enjoy:
- Free coffee and snacks
- Discount prices 30% below our regular low prices!
- Automatic entry in a special prize-giveaway drawing with any purchase!
- A $50 gift card for joining our Frequent Shopper Club!

It's our way of saying "THANK YOU" to our valued customers.

**3.** Where will the event be held?

**(A)** At a movie theater
**(B)** At a restaurant
**(C)** At a public park
**(D)** At a shopping center

**4.** What can a visitor receive without making a purchase?

**(A)** A free drink
**(B)** A free consultation
**(C)** A discount coupon
**(D)** A trial membership

答え合わせの前に、次のページで精読をしましょう！

## 精読タイム！

1語1語に注目しながら、正確に和訳しましょう。

**設問の精読**

3. Where **will** the event **be held**?
   どこでその催しは（　　　　　　　　　　　　）？

4. What **can** a visitor **receive** without making a **purchase**?
   来店者は何を（　　　　　　　　　　　　）、（　　　　　　）することなしに？

**文書の精読** ★重要な部分だけ！

Shay Hardware Outlet **is opening** a new store
Shay Hardware Outlet は、新しい店舗を（　　　　　　　　　　　　）
↑ 注：どんなお店？（　　　　　　　　　　　　）

in the Cranberry Shopping Mall.
Cranberry ショッピングモール内に。

During **the Grand Opening**, ALL VISITORS can enjoy:
（　　　　　　　　　　　　）の間、すべての来場者は以下のものをお楽しみいただけます、

· **Free coffee** and snacks
（　　　　　　　　　　　　）と軽食

**選択肢の精読** ★重要な部分だけ！

4. (B) A free **consultation** 無料の（　　　　　　　　）
   (D) A **trial** membership （　　　　　　　　）会員権

## Reflection

Unit 1 で学んだ単語・表現をチェックしましょう。

意味がすぐに浮かぶようになるまで、反復練習しましょう。

| | | | |
|---|---|---|---|
| ☐ display | ☐ grocery | ☐ clerk | ☐ cashier |
| ☐ arrange | ☐ purchase | ☐ shopper | ☐ reach into |
| ☐ shelf | ☐ discount | ☐ grand opening | ☐ hardware |
| ☐ sign | ☐ in a row | ☐ hang | ☐ browse |
| ☐ measurement | ☐ reality | ☐ difference | ☐ join |
| ☐ competition | ☐ competitor | ☐ drawing | ☐ outlet |

# Unit 2 Office Work

**TOEIC では** ・「オフィスでのやりとり」が題材として多数登場します。

**この Unit では** ・オフィスでよく登場する語句・会話表現・文書などに親しみましょう。
・文法は「形容詞」を深く学びましょう。

## Vocabulary Attack

**1** カタカナ語になっている TOEIC 頻出語句の音声を聞いてリピートし、意味を確認しましょう。 11

| | | | |
|---|---|---|---|
| copy | コピー、部・冊<br>複写する | department | （会社・役所の）部署、部局<br>（店舗の）売り場 |
| schedule | スケジュール、表<br>予定を入れる | tour | ツアー、見学、巡業<br>見学する、旅して回る |
| stock | ストック、在庫<br>蓄える、置いている | recruit | 新規採用する<br>新規採用者 |

**2** その他の TOEIC 頻出語句をマスターしましょう。

❶ まずは音声を聞いてリピートしましょう。 12

| | | | |
|---|---|---|---|
| document | entrance | receptionist | interview |
| colleague | plant | hand out | headquarters |
| conference | client | stairs | drawer |
| greet | bulletin board | representative | present |

❷ 上の表の中から、下線部に適切な英語を選び入れましょう。

| モノ | 人 | 動作 | その他 |
|---|---|---|---|
| 掲示板<br>→ ________ | 顧客<br>→ ________ | 発表する<br>→ ________ | 会議<br>→ ________ |
| 引き出し<br>→ ________ | 同僚<br>→ ________ | 挨拶する<br>→ ________ | 玄関、入り口<br>→ ________ |
| 書類<br>→ ________ | 受付係<br>→ ________ | 配布する<br>→ ________ | 階段<br>→ ________ |
| 植物<br>→ ________ | 担当者<br>→ ________ | 面談・面接（する）<br>→ ________ | 本社<br>→ ________ |

# Part 1 写真問題

**攻略ポイント** 複数の人がいる写真

- 人々の動作や状態、位置関係に注目しましょう。
- 各人がそれぞれバラバラの動作・状態をしている場合は特に注意しましょう。

## Practice 1

**事前に確認** どんな単語を使って写真を表現するか、各自またはペアで思い描きましょう。

例 I see モノ in this picture. / I think she(he) is ～ing. / I think she(he) is in the 場所.

**Step 1** 音声を聞き、写真を正しく描写している選択肢にマークしましょう。 13-15

**Step 2** 再び音声を聞き、空所を埋めてから、もう一度正解を選びましょう。 13-15

**1.**

**Step 1** Ⓐ Ⓑ

**Step 2**

(A) A woman is ( ) a ( ) ( ).

(B) A woman is ( ) some ( ).

**2.**

**Step 1** Ⓐ Ⓑ Ⓒ

**Step 2**

(A) A woman is ( ) a ( )

(B) A man is ( ) on a ( ).

(C) They are ( ) to a ( ).

**3.**

**Step 1** Ⓐ Ⓑ Ⓒ Ⓓ

**Step 2**

(A) They are ( ) a guided ( ).

(B) They are ( ) ( ) some paper.

(C) They are ( ) each other.

(D) They are going ( ) the ( ).

# Part 2 応答問題

**攻略ポイント** WH 疑問文②

- WH 疑問文に加えて、主語や動詞などにも意識を向けましょう。
- 様々な応答パターンに触れ、徐々に慣れていきましょう。

## Practice 2

**Step 1** WH 疑問文を聞いて、WH 疑問詞に○をつけましょう。 16

1. who / when / where / what
2. who / when / where / what
3. who / when / where / what
4. when / where / what / why / which
5. when / where / what / how / which
6. when / where / what / why / how

**Step 2** 同じ英文を聞いて、空所を埋めましょう。 16

1. ( ) is ( ) at today's conference?
2. ( ) can I find the ( ) ( )?
3. ( ) did you ( ) ( ) the bulletin ( )?
4. ( ) do you want to ( ) for lunch today?
5. ( ) ( ) ( ) do you want to buy?
6. ( ) are you going to ( ) your ( )?

## Practice 3

TOEIC 形式（Part 2）の問題を解きましょう。（WH 疑問詞に気を付けて！） 17-19

**Step 1** 正解を選びましょう。　**Step 2** 聞き取れた単語をメモしましょう。

1. Ⓐ Ⓑ Ⓒ
2. Ⓐ Ⓑ Ⓒ
3. Ⓐ Ⓑ Ⓒ

# Part 5 短文穴埋め問題

**攻略ポイント** 品詞問題②形容詞

- 選択肢に、語尾が異なるだけの単語が並んでいたら「品詞問題」と考えましょう。
- 語尾から品詞が判断できるよう、しっかり練習しましょう。
- 空所の前後の品詞も判断できると、正解がより選びやすくなります。

## 文法ポイント 形容詞

- 状態、性質、種類などを表す言葉　例 新しい、長い、重要な、初めての
- 名詞を修飾する　例 new, long, important, first
- 形容詞＋名詞、very+ 形容詞 という形になる　例 **new** clients, very **long**
- 補語になる　例 This client is **important**.
  主語　述語　補語（主語の補足）

- 主な形容詞の語尾の特徴

| | |
|---|---|
| -ful | care**ful**, beauti**ful** |
| -ble | possi**ble**, responsi**ble** |
| -al | form**al**, casu**al** |
| -tory | introduc**tory**, regula**tory** |
| -ve | acti**ve**, positi**ve** |
| -less | care**less**, home**less** |
| 副詞 (-ly) から ly を取ると形容詞 | fond**ly**（副詞）– ly=fond（形容詞） |

（注：例外もあります。arriv**al** 名詞、fact**ory** 名詞など）

## Practice 4

上記の「語尾の特徴」を参考に、次の A ～ D の語の中から**形容詞**を選び、[　　] に**形**と記入しましょう（余裕があれば、**名詞 / 副詞**にも**名・副**と記入しましょう）。

| | A | B | C | D |
|---|---|---|---|---|
| 1 | [　　] nation | [　　] nationally | [　　] nationalize | [　　] national |
| 2 | [　　] full | [　　] fill | [　　] fully | [　　] fulness |
| 3 | [　　] creation | [　　] create | [　　] creative | [　　] creator |
| 4 | [　　] access | [　　] accessible | [　　] accessibility | [　　] accessibly |
| 5 | [　　] annual | [　　] anniversary | [　　] annually | [　　] annualize |

## Practice 5

Practice 4 の単語から、以下の英文に合うものを選んで（　　）に記入しましょう。

1. This database is not (　　　　　　　　) to new recruits.
   使うことができる
2. We expect (　　　　　　　　) attendance at the upcoming online seminar.
   完全な、全員の
3. You will find the essential information in our (　　　　　　　　) report.
   年次の、年に一度の
4. The (　　　　　　　　) competition will take place virtually in April.
   全国的な

## Practice 6

TOEIC 形式（Part 5）の問題です。空欄に入る適切な語を (A) ~ (D) から選びましょう。

解答時間：1 分 30 秒

1. A list of ------- positions can be found on our Web site, which is updated daily.
   - **(A)** avail
   - **(B)** availability
   - **(C)** availably
   - **(D)** available

2. This article says that a navy-blue suit would be ------- for a formal job interview.
   - **(A)** appropriate
   - **(B)** appropriacy
   - **(C)** appropriately
   - **(D)** appropriateness

3. Ms. Evans thanked her colleagues for being very ------- in drawing up the sales plan.
   - **(A)** help
   - **(B)** helped
   - **(C)** helpless
   - **(D)** helpful

# Part 7 読解問題

**攻略ポイント** 社内掲示物

- sign（貼り紙）、notice（通知文）には、様々な注意事項や重要事項が記載されています。
- 細かい点だけではなく、全体から伝わってくる内容（掲示場所、事業内容、施設概要など）にも注意しましょう。

社内の貼り紙（sign）を読みましょう。

**Westerford Consulting Group Ltd.**
**Attention: All Employees**

Please take the following security steps every time you leave the office:

- Log out of your employee account.
- Return all client files to the locked drawers in the storage room.

These steps are essential in order to ensure company network security and to guard against data theft or loss.

—The WCG Security Team

**サンプル設問** ①まずは設問の意味を確認し、②文書からそれらの情報を探しましょう。

1. Where would the sign most likely **be found**?
   - (A) On a product label
   - (B) On an office bulletin board
   - (C) In an annual report
   - (D) In a computer manual

設問の意味
この貼り紙はどこでおそらく（　　　　　　）？

ヒント 文書の最初と最後の部分に注目して考えてみよう。

2. According to the sign, where should client **documents** be **kept**?
   - (A) In a locked box
   - (B) In a filing basket
   - (C) In a display case
   - (D) In a storeroom

設問の意味
この貼り紙によると、どこに顧客の（　　　　　　）は（　　　　　）されるべき？

ヒント client documents について書いている部分と、選択肢を見比べよう。

## Practice 7

読解問題に挑戦しましょう。

**解き方の手順**

1. まずは文書の種類を確認しましょう。 notice ⇒ お知らせ
2. 続いて設問を読んで「何を答えないといけないか」チェックしましょう。
3. 本文だけではなく文書の隅々にまで目を向けましょう。

Questions 3-4 refer to the following notice. 解答時間：2分

***NOTICE: Upcoming Elevator Repair Work***

Due to routine repair work, Elevator No. 2 will be out of service on Friday, November 12. Please use Elevator No. 1, the Service Elevator near the South Entrance of the building. Alternatively, you may use the stairs, accessible from the North Entrance Main Lobby.

Thank you for your patience and cooperation!

—The Stanley Office Towers Maintenance Team

**3.** Why will Elevator No. 2 be out of service on November 12?

**(A)** For a movie shoot
**(B)** For installation of another elevator
**(C)** For a power outage
**(D)** For regular maintenance

**4.** What is indicated about the Stanley Office Towers?

**(A)** They are located near a train station.
**(B)** They have been recently completed.
**(C)** They have more than one entrance.
**(D)** They are available for rent.

答え合わせの前に、次のページで精読をしましょう！

## 精読タイム！

1語1語に注目しながら、正確に和訳しましょう。

### 設問の精読

3. Why will Elevator No. 2 be **out of service** on November 12?
なぜ、2号エレベーターは（　　　　　　　　　　　）、11月12日に？

4. What **is indicated** about the Stanley Office Towers?
何が（　　　　　　　　　　　）、Stanleyオフィスタワーについて？

### 文書の精読

★重要な部分だけ！

Due to **routine repair work**, Elevator No. 2 will be out of service on November 12.
（　　　　　　　　　　　）のため、2号エレベーターは停止します、11月12日に。

Please use Elevator No. 1 near the South **Entrance** of the building.
1号エレベーターを使ってください、ビルの南（　　　　　　）の近くの。

You may use the **stairs**, accessible from the North Entrance Main Lobby.
（　　　　　）を使うこともできます、それには北玄関のメインロビーからアクセスできます。

The Stanley Office Towers **Maintenance** Team
Stanleyオフィスタワー　（　　　　　　　）チーム

### 選択肢の精読

★重要な部分だけ！

3. (B) For **installation** of another elevator　もう1台のエレベーターの（　　　　　）のため
   (D) For regular **maintenance**　定期的な（　　　　　）のため

4. (C) They have **more than one** entrance.　それらには（　　　　　）入り口がある。
   (D) They are available for **rent**.　それらには（　　　　　）用の空きがある。

## Reflection

Unit 2で学んだ単語・表現をチェックしましょう。

意味がすぐに浮かぶようになるまで、反復練習しましょう。

| | | | |
|---|---|---|---|
| ☐ department | ☐ document | ☐ entrance | ☐ receptionist |
| ☐ colleague | ☐ plant | ☐ hand out | ☐ headquarters |
| ☐ conference | ☐ client | ☐ stairs | ☐ drawer |
| ☐ greet | ☐ bulletin board | ☐ representative | ☐ present |
| ☐ accessible | ☐ annual | ☐ available | ☐ appropriate |
| ☐ security | ☐ indicate | ☐ maintenance | ☐ storeroom |

# Unit 3 Transportation

**TOEIC では**
- 様々な「移動手段・交通機関」が題材として多数登場します。

**この Unit では**
- 移動手段・交通機関に関する語句・会話表現・文書などに親しみましょう。
- 文法は「副詞」を深く学びましょう。

## Vocabulary Attack

**1** カタカナ語になっている TOEIC 頻出語句の音声を聞いてリピートし、意味を確認しましょう。 20

| | | | |
|---|---|---|---|
| ticket | チケット、券 | gate | 門、ゲート |
| train | 電車、列車<br>訓練・研修する | platform | 駅のプラットホーム<br>台、壇 |
| book | 本、書籍、予約する | shuttle | 往復運転（シャトルバス） |

**2** その他の TOEIC 頻出語句をマスターしましょう。

❶ まずは音声を聞いてリピートしましょう。 21

| | | | |
|---|---|---|---|
| luggage | board | cross | pedestrian |
| fare | souvenir | load | vehicle |
| commuter | arrival | bound for | express |
| occupied | departure | attendant | passenger |

❷ 上の表の中から、下線部に適切な英語を選び入れましょう。

**モノ**

車両
→ ______________

お土産
→ ______________

旅行手荷物
→ ______________

急行、速達
→ ______________

**人**

乗客
→ ______________

歩行者
→ ______________

係員、案内係
→ ______________

通勤・通学者
→ ______________

**動作・状態**

乗り込む
→ ______________

横断する
→ ______________

埋まっている
→ ______________

~行きである
→ ______________

積み込む
→ ______________

**その他**

出発
→ ______________

到着
→ ______________

運賃
→ ______________

# Part 1 写真問題

**攻略ポイント** モノが中心の写真①

- 人が写っていない写真は、「モノの状態・情景」の描写がポイントになります。
- モノが「～されているところ」なら ⇒ **is (are) ～ ing + 過去分詞**

例 A curtain **is being opened**.（カーテンが開けられているところだ）

## Practice 1

**事前に確認** どんな単語を使って写真を表現するか、各自またはペアで思い描きましょう。

例 I see モノ in this picture. / I think it is ～ . / I think they are in the 場所 .

**Step 1** 音声を聞き、写真を正しく描写している選択肢にマークしましょう。 22-24

**Step 2** 再び音声を聞き、空所を埋めてから、もう一度正解を選びましょう。 22-24

**1.**

**Step 1** Ⓐ Ⓑ

**Step 2**

(A) Some (　　　　) is placed on a (　　　　).

(B) Some (　　　　) are being loaded into a (　　　　).

**2.**

**Step 1** Ⓐ Ⓑ Ⓒ

**Step 2**

(A) Some (　　　　) are (　　　　) a (　　　　).

(B) (　　　　) are not (　　　　).

(C) (　　　　) are (　　　　) on a (　　　　).

**3.**

**Step 1** Ⓐ Ⓑ Ⓒ Ⓓ

**Step 2**

(A) (　　　　) are (　　　　) alongside a wall.

(B) (　　　　) are (　　　　) to each other.

(C) (　　　　) are (　　　　) a bridge.

(D) (　　　　) are pulling (　　　　).

# Part 2 応答問題

**攻略ポイント** 勧誘・提案①

WH 疑問詞から始まる文でも、疑問文ではなく「勧誘・提案」の表現があります。

- **Why don't you** + 動詞？ **あなた**～したらどうですか？（しませんか？）
- **Why don't we** + 動詞？ **一緒に**～しませんか？（しましょうよ。）

★ **Why** の中でも **don't you / don't we** のときだけなので、気を付けましょう。

## Practice 2

**Step 1** WH 疑問文を聞いて、WH 疑問詞に〇をつけましょう。 25

1. who / when / where / what
2. who / when / where / why
3. who / when / where / what
4. when / where / what / why / which
5. when / where / what / why / which
6. when / where / what / why / which

**Step 2** 同じ英文を聞いて、空所を埋めましょう。 25

1. (　　　　) will (　　　　　　) (　　　　)?
2. (　　　　) was the morning (　　　　) (　　　　　　)?
3. (　　　　) (　　　　) does the (　　　　) (　　　　) for Boston?
4. (　　　　) (　　　　) is (　　　　　　) at the moment?
5. (　　　　) (　　　　) you (　　　　) a round-trip (　　　　)?
6. (　　　　) can I (　　　　) some (　　　　　　　　)?

## Practice 3

TOEIC 形式（Part 2）の問題を解きましょう。 26-28

**Step 1** 正解を選びましょう。　**Step 2** 聞き取れた単語をメモしましょう。

1. Ⓐ Ⓑ Ⓒ
2. Ⓐ Ⓑ Ⓒ
3. Ⓐ Ⓑ Ⓒ

# Part 5 短文穴埋め問題

**攻略ポイント** 品詞問題③副詞

- 選択肢に、語尾が異なるだけの単語が並んでいたら「品詞問題」と考えましょう。
- 語尾から品詞が判断できるよう、しっかり練習しましょう。
- 修飾関係が見えてくると、さらに正解が選びやすくなります。

**文法ポイント** 副詞

- 名詞**以外の語句**を修飾する　例 **すぐに**出発する、**非常に**重要な
  - 復習 名詞を修飾するのは⇒ [　　　　] 詞
- 文を修飾するものもある（接続副詞）　例 **その上**、電車は遅れていた。
- [副詞] + [形容詞・副詞・動詞など] という形になる　例 **simply** wonderful, **very** slowly
- 文頭や文尾に置かれることも多い　例 Please talk **slowly**. / **Simply** call this number.
- 主な副詞の語尾の特徴：**-ly**（形容詞＋ ly ＝副詞）
  （注：例外もあります。time**ly** 形容詞、cost**ly** 形容詞など）
- それ以外の主な副詞

| | | | |
|---|---|---|---|
| very | とても | yet | まだ |
| already | 既に | always | いつも |
| hard ※ | 熱心に | never | 決して～ない |
| almost | ほぼ、もう少しで | often | しばしば |

※ hard は形容詞にもなる（熱心な）

## Practice 4

上記の「語尾の特徴」を参考に、次の A ～ D の語の中から**形容詞 / 副詞**を選び、[ ] に**形 / 副**と記入しましょう（余裕があれば、**名詞**にも**名**と記入しましょう）。

| | A | B | C | D |
|---|---|---|---|---|
| 1 | [　] sharp | [　] sharpness | [　] sharpen | [　] sharply |
| 2 | [　] accurate | [　] accuracy | [　] accurately | [　] accurateness |
| 3 | [　] extend | [　] extensive | [　] extension | [　] extensively |
| 4 | [　] functionally | [　] functional | [　] functionality | [　] function |
| 5 | [　] generality | [　] generally | [　] generalize | [　] general |

## Practice 5

Practice 4 の単語から、以下の英文に合うものを選んで（　　）に記入しましょう。
（注：今回は、形容詞か副詞か検討し、適切な品詞を選ぶ必要があります）

1. Stock prices have increased (　　　　　　　　) in recent months.
急激に

2. These two smartphones look similar, but they are (　　　　　　　　) different.
機能的には

3. Local maps are (　　　　　　　　) provided for free at tourist information centers.
概して、一般的に

4. We conducted an (　　　　　　　　) survey on customer satisfaction.
大規模な・徹底的な

## Practice 6

TOEIC 形式（Part 5）の問題です。空欄に入る適切な語を (A) ~ (D) から選びましょう。

解答時間：1 分 30 秒

1. Ada Stewart, a prominent novelist, has been writing ------- for the last ten years.
   (A) profession
   (B) professional
   (C) professionally
   (D) professionalism

2. A ------- number of attendees stayed after the session for a photo shoot.
   (A) considered
   (B) considerably
   (C) consider
   (D) considerable

3. The manager has ------- asked his staff to submit app development ideas.
   (A) repeat
   (B) repeatedly
   (C) repeated
   (D) repetition

# Part 7 読解問題

**攻略ポイント** リストを含む掲示物

- タイトルに注目して、何を表す掲示物なのか判断しましょう。
- リスト（表）の項目に目を向けて、何がリストアップされているか確認しましょう。
- リスト（表）の上・下にも重要な情報が書いてあるので忘れずに読みましょう。

乗り物に関する掲示物（sign）を読みましょう。

Tired of Traffic? Take the Ferry to and from Port Pico

**Ticket prices for the Port Pico Ferry service**

| Ferry Route | One Way | Round Trip |
|---|---|---|
| Oak City | $9 | $17 |
| Kelly | $8 | $15 |
| Hollytown | $8 | $15 |
| Bay Heights | $3 | $5 |

- Children aged 12 and under ride for free.
- All passengers may board with bicycles for a fee of $1 for each bicycle each way.
- No motor vehicle service. Use the Freighter Ferry service if you are traveling with your car.

**サンプル設問** ①まずは設問の意味を確認し、②文書からそれらの情報を探しましょう。

1. How much is a **round-trip** ticket between Bay Heights and Port Pico?
   (A) 3 dollars
   (B) 5 dollars
   (C) 9 dollars
   (D) 15 dollars

**設問の意味**
いくらですか？ Bay Heights と Port Pico の間の
(　　　　　　　　) のチケットは？

**ヒント** 表の上や中身から、該当する情報を探そう。

2. What **is indicated** about the Port Pico Ferry service?
   (A) It has a group discount.
   (B) It sponsors a bike race.
   (C) It will change its fares soon.
   (D) It does not load cars.

**設問の意味**
Port Pico Ferry について、
何が（　　　　　　　　）？

**ヒント** 表の下に書いている注意書きから検討しよう。

## Practice 7

読解問題に挑戦しましょう。

**解き方の手順**

1. まずは文書の種類を確認しましょう。 notice ⇒ お知らせ
2. 続いて設問を読んで「何を答えないといけないか」チェックしましょう。
3. 本文だけではなく文書の隅々にまで目を向けましょう。

Questions 3-4 refer to the following notice.

解答時間：2分

### Scheduled Northbound Stops for Bus Route No. 72
### Kensing Terminal ⇒ Central Station

| Bus Stop Names | First / Last Departure Times |
|---|---|
| Kensing Terminal | 6:00 a.m. / 10:00 p.m. |
| 34th Avenue | 6:15 a.m. / 10:15 p.m. |
| Postal Center | 6:27 a.m. / 10:27 p.m. |
| Galley Hill Mall | 6:35 a.m. / 10:35 p.m. |
| St. John Hospital | 6:41 a.m. / 10:41 p.m. |

➡ The bus does not run on weekends or holidays.

➡ For real-time schedule updates, use your smartphone to scan the code posted at each bus stop.

3. At what time is a bus scheduled to leave Galley Hill Mall?
   (A) 10:00 p.m.
   (B) 10:15 p.m.
   (C) 10:35 p.m.
   (D) 10:41 p.m.

4. According to the notice, what is true about Bus Route No. 72?
   (A) The service is not available on Sundays.
   (B) A schedule update is provided every hour.
   (C) Passengers can use smartphones to buy tickets.
   (D) Commuter passes can be purchased on board.

答え合わせの前に、次のページで精読をしましょう！

## 精読タイム！

1語1語に注目しながら、正確に和訳しましょう。

### 設問の精読

3. At what time is a bus **scheduled to leave** Galley Hill Mall?
何時に、バスは Galley Hill Mall を（　　　　　　　　　　　　）？

4. **According to** the notice, what is **true** about Bus Route No. 72?
お知らせ（　　　　　　　　　　）、何が（　　　　　）ですか、72番のバス路線について？

### 文書の精読　★重要な部分だけ！

Scheduled North**bound** Stops for Bus Route No. 72
72番のバス路線の北（　　　　）の停車予定（場所＆時刻）

The bus does not **run** on **weekends** or holidays.
このバスは（　　　　）しません、（　　　　）や祝日は。

For real-time schedule **updates**, **use** your smartphone
運行時間のリアルタイムな（　　　　）を見るには、スマートフォンを（　　　　　　　　　　）、

to **scan** the code posted at each bus stop.
各バス停に掲示されているコードを（　　　　　　　　　　）ために。

### 選択肢の精読　★重要な部分だけ！

4. (A) The service is not **available** on Sundays.
このサービスは（　　　　　）できない、日曜は。

(B) A schedule update is provided **every hour**.
運行スケジュールの更新は、（　　　　　）ごとに行われる。

## Reflection

Unit 3 で学んだ単語・表現をチェックしましょう。

意味がすぐに浮かぶようになるまで、反復練習しましょう。

| | | | |
|---|---|---|---|
| ☐ luggage | ☐ board | ☐ cross | ☐ pedestrian |
| ☐ fare | ☐ souvenir | ☐ load | ☐ vehicle |
| ☐ commuter | ☐ arrival | ☐ bound for | ☐ express |
| ☐ occupied | ☐ departure | ☐ attendant | ☐ passenger |
| ☐ platform | ☐ sharply | ☐ extensive | ☐ functionality |
| ☐ generally | ☐ considerable | ☐ round-trip | ☐ available |

# Unit 4 Travel & Eating Out

**TOEIC では** • 様々な「旅行・出張」「外食」の場面が題材として多数登場します。

**この Unit では** • 旅行・出張や外食の場面によく登場する語句・会話表現・文書などに親しみましょう。
• 文法は「動詞（述語動詞の基本）」を学びましょう。

## Vocabulary Attack

**1** カタカナ語になっている TOEIC 頻出語句の音声を聞いてリピートし、意味を確認しましょう。 A 29

| | | | |
|---|---|---|---|
| hotel | ホテル | cancel | キャンセルする、中止する |
| set | セット（ひとそろい）<br>設置する | rest | 休憩、休憩する<br>（腕、頬などを）載せる、置く |
| ride | ライド（乗車、乗ること）<br>乗る | buffet | ビュッフェ（バイキング）、<br>セルフサービス形式の食事 |

**2** その他の TOEIC 頻出語句をマスターしましょう。

❶ まずは音声を聞いてリピートしましょう。 A 30

| | | | |
|---|---|---|---|
| seating | landmark | reserve | housekeeper |
| agent | admission | exhibition | beverage |
| overlook | fountain | meal | itinerary |
| accommodation | pick up | server | reception |

❷ 上の表の中から、下線部に適切な英語を選び入れましょう。

| モノ | 人 | 動作 | その他 |
|---|---|---|---|
| 食事<br>→ ________ | 代理・仲介業者<br>→ ________ | 迎えに行く、受け取る<br>→ ________ | 宿泊<br>→ ________ |
| 飲み物<br>→ ________ | 客室係<br>→ ________ | 見下ろす、見渡す<br>→ ________ | 受付、歓迎・祝賀会<br>→ ________ |
| 名所、旧跡<br>→ ________ | 給仕係<br>→ ________ | 予約する、取り置きする<br>→ ________ | 入会、入場<br>→ ________ |
| 座席<br>→ ________ | 噴水、泉<br>→ ________ | 旅程<br>→ ________ | 展示会<br>→ ________ |

# Part 1 写真問題

**攻略ポイント** モノが中心の写真②

- 人が写っていない写真は、「モノの状態・情景」の描写がポイントになります。
- モノが「〜にある」なら ⇒ **There is (are) ＋名詞＋場所**

例 **There is** a laptop on the desk.（机の上にノートパソコンがある）

## Practice 1

**事前に確認** どんな単語を使って写真を表現するか、各自またはペアで思い描きましょう。

例 There is (are) **モノ** in this picture. / I think it's (they're) in the **場所**.

**Step 1** 音声を聞き、写真を正しく描写している選択肢にマークしましょう。 A 31-33

**Step 2** 再び音声を聞き、空所を埋めてから、もう一度正解を選びましょう。 A 31-33

1.

**Step 1** Ⓐ Ⓑ

**Step 2**

(A) A (　　　) has been (　　　　　) on the table.

(B) A balcony (　　　　　) a (　　　).

2.

**Step 1** Ⓐ Ⓑ Ⓒ

**Step 2**

(A) There is some (　　　　) (　　　　).

(B) (　　　　) are (　　　　) tables.

(C) The dining (　　　) is (　　　　　).

3.

**Step 1** Ⓐ Ⓑ Ⓒ Ⓓ

**Step 2**

(A) People are (　　　　) in a (　　　) (　　　).

(B) There are some chairs (　　　　) a (　　　　).

(C) Umbrellas are (　　　　) on a (　　　).

(D) Some (　　　) are being (　　　) in the park.

# Part 2 応答問題

**攻略ポイント** 勧誘・提案②

- WH 疑問詞から始まる文でも、疑問文ではなく**「勧誘・提案」**の表現があります。Unit 3 で学習した「Why don't you / we ～ ?」に追加して、この Unit では以下の表現を学びましょう。
- **How about** + 名詞？　～はどうですか？ / いかがですか？
- **How about** + 動名詞（～ ing）？　～したらどうですか？ / しませんか？

## Practice 2

**Step 1** WH 疑問文を聞いて、WH 疑問詞に○をつけましょう。　34

1. who / when / where / what
2. who / when / where / which
3. who / when / where / how
4. who / where / what / why / which
5. when / where / what / why / which
6. when / where / what / why / how

**Step 2** 同じ英文を聞いて、空所を埋めましょう。　34

1. (　　　) is the special (　　　　　　) being (　　　)?
2. (　　　) caterer did you (　　　) for the (　　　　　　)?
3. (　　　) (　　　) sharing a (　　　) with me to the airport?
4. (　　　) usually makes (　　　) (　　　　　) for you?
5. (　　　) do you (　　　) a (　　　)-style breakfast?
6. (　　　) (　　　) is (　　　　　　) if we make reservations early?

## Practice 3

TOEIC 形式（Part 2）の問題を解きましょう。　35-37

**Step 1** 正解を選びましょう。　**Step 2** 聞き取れた単語をメモしましょう。

1. Ⓐ Ⓑ Ⓒ
2. Ⓐ Ⓑ Ⓒ
3. Ⓐ Ⓑ Ⓒ

# Part 5 短文穴埋め問題

**攻略ポイント** 動詞①述語動詞の基本

- 動詞は、他の品詞とは異なり、様々に形を変化させます。
- 正しい形を選ぶためのポイントをしっかり押さえましょう。
- まずは述語（V）になる形をしっかり学びましょう。

**文法ポイント** **動詞**

- 人・物・事の**動作**や**状態**などについて述べる語　例 smile, break, happen
- 述語（V）になる用法と、ならない用法がある（本書では前者を中心に学ぶ）
- 述語（V）になる＝**述語動詞になる**形

［基本形］**go** という動詞を、形を変えて入れてみましょう。

| | | | |
|---|---|---|---|
| 現在形 | go / goes | 過去形 | (　　　　) |
| be 動詞＋現在分詞（進行形） | is (　　　　) | be 動詞＋過去分詞（受動態） | are (　　　　) |
| 助動詞＋原形 | will (　　　　) | have+ 過去分詞（完了形） | have (　　　　) |

- 主な動詞の語尾の特徴　※ 例外もあります。puf**fy** 形容詞、woo**den** 形容詞など

| | | | |
|---|---|---|---|
| -fy | noti**fy**, clari**fy** | -ze | reali**ze**, analy**ze** |
| -ate | cre**ate**, oper**ate** | -en | sharp**en**, sweet**en** |

迷ったら
- 一番「短い語」が動詞のことが比較的多い。
  例 add / additional / addition　⇒動詞は？［　　　　］
- 語尾が **-ing** /**-(e)d** ⇒それを取れば動詞の原形（もしくは現在形）
  例 remain**ing** / depart**ed**

## Practice 4

上記の「語尾の特徴」を参考に、次の A ~ D の語の中から**名詞 / 動詞 / 形容詞 / 副詞**を選び、［ ］に**名 / 動 / 形 / 副**と記入しましょう（Unit 1 ~ 3 の復習も兼ねています）。

| | A | B | C | D |
|---|---|---|---|---|
| 1 | [　　] satisfaction | [　　] satisfactory | [　　] satisfactorily | [　　] satisfy |
| 2 | [　　] appreciate | [　　] appreciation | [　　] appreciative | [　　] appreciatively |
| 3 | [　　] customer | [　　] customize | [　　] customary | [　　] customization |
| 4 | [　　] wide | [　　] widely | [　　] widen | [　　] wideness |

## Practice 5

Practice 4 の単語から、以下の英文に合うものを選び、適切な形に変えて（　　）に記入しましょう。
※ ここでは「時」や「前後の語（be 動詞、助動詞など）」を考慮して、形を変化させる必要があります。

1. You must (　　　　　　　　) certain requirements to become a receptionist.
満たす

2. We (　　　　　　　　) the main street and add a bike lane early next year.
広げる

3. The chef (　　　　　　　　) a menu for us as some of the guests were vegetarian.
合わせて作る

4. Any contribution to this charity will be gratefully (　　　　　　　　).
感謝される

## Practice 6

TOEIC 形式（Part 5）の問題です。空欄に入る適切な語を (A) ~ (D) から選びましょう。

解答時間：1 分 30 秒

1. The staff ------- a new dishwasher after the plumber repaired the water pipe.
   - **(A)** install
   - **(B)** installed
   - **(C)** installing
   - **(D)** installation

2. The Beatrix art museum in Liverpool ------- its doors to the public in two weeks.
   - **(A)** will open
   - **(B)** opened
   - **(C)** opening
   - **(D)** has opened

3. Mr. Gupta is ------- suited for the new marketing position in Singapore.
   - **(A)** perfect
   - **(B)** perfection
   - **(C)** perfected
   - **(D)** perfectly

# Part 7 読解問題

**攻略ポイント** Eメール

- From / To：差出人・受取人の氏名の他に、ドメイン名（@～）にも注目。所属先等がわかります。
  ⇒本文冒頭の「Dear ～（受取人)」＆本文最後の「署名（差出人)」でも情報収集できます。
- Subject（主題）←概要がつかめます。
- Date（日付）←問題を解く鍵になることもあります。

旅行予定について伝える「Eメール」を読みましょう。

From: Guest Services <GuestServices@EavesBeachHotels.com>
To: Sarah Tyler <styler9873@mailease.com>
Subject: Reservation
Date: June 9, 2:11 P.M.

---

Dear Ms. Tyler,

Thank you for reserving a room at the Eaves Beach Inn for the nights of July 7 and 8. For your convenience, we recommend that you visit www.EavesBeachHotels.com to complete the online check-in and confirmation process before you arrive.

If there is anything we can help you with before you arrive, please do not hesitate to call the Guest Services Center at 555-234-9879 any time.

Guest Services Team, Eaves Beach Inn
341 Ocean Drive, Ross Beach, CA

**サンプル設問** ①まずは設問の意味を確認し、②文書からそれらの情報を探しましょう。

1. What **is indicated** about Ms. Tyler's **reservation**?
   (A) It was made by phone.
   (B) It was made two days ago.
   (C) It is for two rooms.
   (D) It is for two nights.

**設問の意味**
Tyler さんの（　　　　）について
何と（　　　　　　　　）？

**ヒント** Ms.Tyler とは？　Eメールの【差出人?受取人?】

2. How can Ms. Tyler **contact** the Guest Services Center?
   (A) In person
   (B) By online chat
   (C) By telephone
   (D) By text message

**設問の意味**
Tyler さんはどうやって（　　　　　　）できますか、
Guest Services Center に？

**ヒント** Guest Services Center というキーワードをEメールから探そう。

## Practice 7

読解問題に挑戦しましょう。

**解き方の手順**

1. まずは文書の種類を確認しましょう。 e-mail ⇒ E メール
2. 続いて設問を読んで「何を答えないといけないか」チェックしましょう。
3. 本文だけではなく文書の隅々にまで目を向けましょう。

Questions 3-4 refer to the following e-mail.

解答時間：2分

To: Armon Gannon <agannon@gralva-corp.com>
From: Regina Fleming <rfleming@gralva-corp.com>
Subject: Chicago Flight Information
Date: Nov. 18, 4:43 P.M.
Attachment: Mr. Gannon's itinerary

---

Mr. Gannon,

I have booked a reservation for you on Acadia Airlines, Flight 403, departing New Jersey for Chicago on Thursday, November 29 at 10:30 A.M. The airline advises arriving at the airport two hours before departure. You can pick up your departure and return tickets at the Acadia Airlines ticket counter. I have attached your airline and hotel reservation information.

See you here in Chicago on Thursday.

Regina Fleming
Convention Project Team

**3.** Why was the e-mail sent?

(A) To inform Mr. Gannon of a schedule change
(B) To cancel a hotel reservation
(C) To book a flight to New Jersey
(D) To provide travel information

**4.** What is suggested about Ms. Fleming?

(A) She lives in Chicago.
(B) She works for an airline company.
(C) She has attached tickets to the e-mail.
(D) She met Mr. Gannon at the airport.

答え合わせの前に、次のページで精読をしましょう！

## 精読タイム！

1語1語に注目しながら、正確に和訳しましょう。

### 設問の精読

3. Why **was** the e-mail **sent**?
   なぜ、Eメールは（　　　　　　　　　）？

4. What **is suggested** about Ms. Fleming?
   Ms. Fleming について何が（　　　　　　　　　）？

### 文書の精読 ★重要な部分だけ！

I have **booked a reservation** for you on Acadia Airlines, Flight 403,
私はあなたのために（　　　　　　　　　）、Acadia 航空 403 便を、

**departing** New Jersey for Chicago on Thursday, November 29 at 10:30 A.M.
（その便は）New Jersey からシカゴに向けて（　　　　　　）、11/29（木）午前 10：30 に。

I have **attached** your airline and hotel reservation information.
私は（　　　　　　　）、航空便とホテルの予約情報を。

See you here in Chicago on Thursday.
ここシカゴでお会いしましょう、木曜日に。

### 選択肢の精読 ★重要な部分だけ！

3. (A) To **inform** Mr. Gannon of a schedule change
   Gannon さんに予定変更を（　　　　　　）ため

   (D) To **provide** travel information
   旅の情報を（　　　　　　）するため

## Reflection

Unit 4 で学んだ単語・表現をチェックしましょう。

意味がすぐに浮かぶようになるまで、反復練習しましょう。

| | | | |
|---|---|---|---|
| □ seating | □ landmark | □ reserve | □ ride |
| □ agent | □ admission | □ exhibition | □ beverage |
| □ overlook | □ fountain | □ meal | □ buffet |
| □ accommodation | □ pick up | □ server | □ reception |
| □ facing | □ How about | □ I'm afraid | □ satisfy |
| □ customize | □ appreciate | □ suggest | □ inform |

# Unit 5 Meetings

**TOEIC では**
- 様々な目的の「会議、会合、集まり」が題材として多数登場します。

**この Unit では**
- 「会議、会合、集まり」に関する語句・会話表現・文書などに親しみましょう。
- 文法は「動詞」を更に深く学びましょう。

## Vocabulary Attack

**1** カタカナ語になっている TOEIC 頻出語句の音声を聞いてリピートし、意味を確認しましょう。 38

| | | | |
|---|---|---|---|
| address | 住所、スピーチ、話しかける | break | 休憩、壊す、壊れる |
| microphone | マイク | projector | プロジェクター、投影機 |
| screen | 画面、幕 | session | （目的のある）集まり、会合 |

**2** その他の TOEIC 頻出語句をマスターしましょう。

❶ まずは音声を聞いてリピートしましょう。 39

| | | | |
|---|---|---|---|
| gather | minutes | workshop | equipment |
| furniture | participant | keynote speaker | register |
| organizer | agenda | refreshments | material |
| lead | attend | presenter | conduct |

❷ 上の表の中から、下線部に適切な英語を選び入れましょう。

**モノ**

家具
→ ________________

軽い飲食物
→ ________________

資料
→ ________________

機器・装置
→ ________________

**人**

参加者
→ ________________

運営係
→ ________________

発表者
→ ________________

基調講演者
→ ________________

**動作**

集まる、集める
→ ________________

行う、実施する
→ ________________

出席する
→ ________________

（参加）登録する
→ ________________

率いる、導く
→ ________________

**その他**

議題、議事項目
→ ________________

講習会、研修会
→ ________________

会議の記録
→ ________________

# Part 1　写真問題

**攻略ポイント**　人やモノの位置関係

- 位置関係を表す語句に注意しましょう。

| | | | | | |
|---|---|---|---|---|---|
| on | ～に接して | in front of | ～の前に | around | ～の周りに |
| above | ～の上方に | behind | ～の後ろに | between | ～の間に |
| under | ～の下に | next to | ～の隣に | by | ～のそばに |

## Practice 1

**事前に確認**　どんな単語を使って写真を表現するか、各自またはペアで思い描きましょう。

例 I see モノ in this picture. / There is(are) モノ + 場所を表す語句 .

**Step 1**　音声を聞き、写真を正しく描写している選択肢にマークしましょう。　A 40-42

**Step 2**　再び音声を聞き、空所を埋めてから、もう一度正解を選びましょう。　A 40-42

**1.**

**Step 1**　Ⓐ Ⓑ

**Step 2**

(A) A (　　　　) is (　　　　) (　　　　) chairs.

(B) Some (　　　　) is being (　　　　).

**2.**

**Step 1**　Ⓐ Ⓑ Ⓒ

**Step 2**

(A) A (　　　　) is adjusting a (　　　　).

(B) People have (　　　　) (　　　　) a table.

(C) A screen is (　　) up in (　　　　) of a (　　　　).

**3.**

**Step 1**　Ⓐ Ⓑ Ⓒ Ⓓ

**Step 2**

(A) A man is (　　　　) out some (　　　　).

(B) Some people are seated (　) to a (　　　).

(C) A man is (　　　　) some office (　　　　　　).

(D) Some (　　　　) are (　　) a buffet table.

# Part 2 応答問題

**攻略ポイント** 依頼・許可

- 助動詞を使った「依頼」「許可を求める」表現が出題されます。
- この２つの意味の聞き分けを意識しましょう。

**押さえておきたい助動詞の表現①**

主語に注目！

| あなたにお願いできる？（依頼） | 私、やっていい？（許可を求める） |
|---|---|
| Can **you** ～？　Could **you** ～？ | Can **I** ～？　Could **I** ～？ |
| Will **you**[*1] ～？　Would **you**[*2] ～？ | May **I** ～？ |

*1 Will you ～？は「～する予定ですか、つもりですか」と尋ねる意味にもなる。
*2 Would you ～？は後ろに like を付けると別の意味になる（次の Unit 以降で学びます）。

## Practice 2

**Step 1** 助動詞から始まる文を聞いて、意味に○をつけましょう。　43

1. 依頼 / 許可を求める
2. 依頼 / 許可を求める
3. 依頼 / 許可を求める
4. 依頼 / 許可を求める
5. 依頼 / 許可を求める
6. 依頼 / 許可を求める

**Step 2** 同じ英文を聞いて、空所を埋めましょう。　43

1. (　　　　) (　　　　) (　　　　) me move a projector?
2. (　　　　) (　　　　) give the opening (　　　　　　)?
3. (　　　　) (　　　　) (　　　　　　) your microphone for a while?
4. (　　　　) (　　　　) (　　　　) an online (　　　　　　)?
5. (　　　　) (　　　　) (　　　　) the meeting (　　　　　　)？
6. (　　　　) (　　　　) (　　　　) me if you have a short (　　　　)?

## Practice 3

TOEIC 形式（Part 2）の問題を解きましょう。　44-46

**Step 1** 正解を選びましょう。　**Step 2** 聞き取れた単語をメモしましょう。

1. Ⓐ Ⓑ Ⓒ
2. Ⓐ Ⓑ Ⓒ
3. Ⓐ Ⓑ Ⓒ

# Part 5 短文穴埋め問題

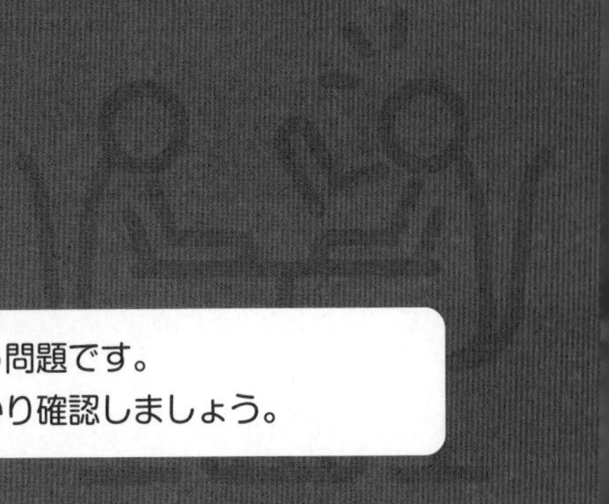

**攻略ポイント** 動詞②態

- 選択肢に、「動詞」が様々な形で並んでいたら「動詞の用法」を問う問題です。
- 頻出項目の１つが態（「～する」「～される」）です。注意点をしっかり確認しましょう。

**文法ポイント** **動詞の「態」**

- **能動態**「～する」 例 We **hold** the meeting. / I **asked** the question.
- **受動態**「～される」（受け身）（be 動詞＋過去分詞） 例 The meeting **is held**. / The question **was asked**.

能動態か受動態か判断するには
①主語 (S) を基準に意味で考える。「**主語が・は**」**～する⇒能動態、～される⇒受動態**
②意味で判断できない場合は、述語の後ろに「**目的語（～を）**」になる**名詞のかたまり**があるかどうかチェック ⇒ 「**ある**」なら**能動態**の可能性が**高い**。
例 He [ attended / was attended ] a gaming conference.
例 He [ invited / was invited ] to speak at a gaming conference.

- 主な「過去分詞」の語形変化

| | |
|---|---|
| **過去形と同じ** | hold – **held** – **held** |
| **原形と同じ** | **run** – ran – **run** |
| **-n** | break – broke – broke**n** |
| **全部同じ** | **put** – **put** – **put** |
| **その他** | drink – dr**a**nk – dr**u**nk |

## Practice 4

今までに学んだ「語尾の特徴」を参考に、次の A ～ D の語の中から**名詞 / 動詞 / 形容詞 / 副詞**を選び、[ ] に**名 / 動 / 形 / 副**と記入しましょう。

| | A | B | C | D |
|---|---|---|---|---|
| 1 | [ ] expansion | [ ] expandable | [ ] expand | [ ] expansively |
| 2 | [ ] develop | [ ] development | [ ] developer | [ ] developmental |
| 3 | [ ] generate | [ ] generation | [ ] generative | [ ] generator |
| 4 | [ ] removal | [ ] removable | [ ] remove | [ ] remover |

## Practice 5

Practice 4 の単語から、以下の英文に合うものを選び、適切な形に変えて（　）に記入しましょう。
※ ここでは「態」「時」「前後の語（be 動詞、助動詞）」などを考慮して、形を変化させる必要があります。

1. A start-up company successfully (　　　　　　　　) this software a year ago.
   開発する

2. One of the artworks (　　　　　　　　) from the exhibition hall last week.
   取り除く

3. The coffee market is rapidly (　　　　　　　　) in Southeast Asia and Africa.
   拡大する

4. It is expected that new jobs will soon (　　　　　　　　) in the IT industry.
   生み出す

## Practice 6

TOEIC 形式（Part 5）の問題です。空欄に入る適切な語を (A) ~ (D) から選びましょう。

解答時間：1 分 30 秒

1. The director ------- an interview with a classical guitarist for the upcoming radio show.
   **(A)** scheduling
   **(B)** was scheduled
   **(C)** to schedule
   **(D)** scheduled

2. There are several conference rooms on this floor, and right now only one room -------.
   **(A)** occupied
   **(B)** occupying
   **(C)** is occupied
   **(D)** occupies

3. York University ------- a special award for its contribution to the local community.
   **(A)** will receive
   **(B)** receiving
   **(C)** was received
   **(D)** to receive

# Part 7 読解問題

**攻略ポイント** 一斉送信メール・通知

- 複数の受取人に向けた E メールや通知文も題材としてよく登場します。
- 「To」欄を見れば、どんな人（所属部署や立場など）が受取人かわかります。
- 差出人はリーダー的な人物で、指示や依頼をする内容が多いという傾向があります。その点に気を付けて読みましょう。

一斉送信された「E メール」を読みましょう。

From: Kathryn Culls <kculls@rivera-comp-d.com>
To: Project Team
Date: Feb. 23, 9:33 A.M.
Subject: Harroldson's Project

As you know, our first weekly meeting for the Harroldson's Corp. cloud computing system project was held last Friday. Since some of you weren't there on Friday, let me remind you that the whole team must attend every meeting. On Friday, we reviewed the client's issues and our solutions. This coming Friday, we will talk about the role that each team member will play in the project. I look forward to seeing all of you then.

Kathryn Culls

Project Manager, Cloud Solutions, RiveraComp. Inc.

**サンプル設問** ①まずは設問の意味を確認し、②文書からそれらの情報を探しましょう。

1. **What is indicated** about the previous meeting?
   (A) It was longer than usual.
   (B) Ms. Culls canceled it.
   (C) Some members did not attend.
   (D) It was held online.

**設問の意味**
前回の会議について
(　　　　　　　　　　　　　　)？

**ヒント** 過去形で書かれている部分に注目。

2. What **will** they **discuss** at the next meeting?
   (A) The client's issues
   (B) Registration fees
   (C) Team-building workshops
   (D) Members' responsibilities

**設問の意味**
次の会議では、彼らは何について
(　　　　　　　　　　)？

**ヒント** will など、未来の時制で書かれている部分に注目。

## Practice 7

読解問題に挑戦しましょう。

**解き方の手順**

1. まずは文書の種類を確認しましょう。 e-mail ⇒ E メール
2. 続いて設問を読んで「何を答えないといけないか」チェックしましょう。
3. 本文だけではなく文書の隅々にまで目を向けましょう。

Questions 3-4 refer to the following e-mail.

解答時間：2 分

From: Stan Wilford
To: Conference Presenters
Date: April 29
Subject: Package Design Conference

---

A quick note on our upcoming conference in June: It is particularly important that each presenter keep their presentation time to 25 minutes or less, including question-and-answer sessions. When your scheduled in-person presentation time is over, there will be an online virtual chat and conference space available for each presenter. If you wish, you can continue the discussion with participants there. Complete details will be provided early next month.

Stan Wilford

3. What is indicated about Mr. Wilford?
   (A) He will present his findings.
   (B) He is organizing a conference.
   (C) He is a Web designer.
   (D) He is a keynote speaker.

4. According to the e-mail, what will Mr. Wilford provide in May?
   (A) Conference programs
   (B) Presentation materials
   (C) Meeting minutes
   (D) Information about virtual spaces

答え合わせの前に、次のページで精読をしましょう！

## 精読タイム！

1語1語に注目しながら、正確に和訳しましょう。

### 設問の精読

**3.** What **is indicated** about Mr. Wilford?
Mr. Wilford について、何（　　　　　　　　　　）？

**4.** According to the e-mail, what will Mr. Wilford **provide** in May?
このEメールによると、Mr. Wilford は5月に何を（　　　　　　　　）予定？

### 文書の精読

★重要な部分だけ！

From: Stan Wilford ⇒【差出人?・受取人?】

To: Conference **Presenters** ⇒ 会議の（　　　　　　　　　）【差出人?・受取人?】

Date: April 29 ⇒【発信日】

A quick note on our **upcoming** conference in June:
私たちの6月に（　　　　　　　　　　）会議についての手短なお知らせです。

**When** your scheduled in-person presentation time is **over**,
あなたがたの予定されている対面での発表時間が（　　　　　　　　　　）、
there will be an online virtual chat and **conference** space
オンラインでのバーチャルチャットと（　　　　　　　　）スペースが用意されます、
**available** for each presenter.
（それは）各発表者が（　　　　　　　　　　）です。

Complete **details** will be provided early next month.
完全な（　　　　　　　　）は、提供されます、来月初旬に。

## Reflection

Unit 5 で学んだ単語・表現をチェックしましょう。

意味がすぐに浮かぶようになるまで、反復練習しましょう。

| | | | |
|---|---|---|---|
| ☐ gather | ☐ minutes | ☐ workshop | ☐ equipment |
| ☐ furniture | ☐ participant | ☐ keynote speaker | ☐ register |
| ☐ organizer | ☐ agenda | ☐ refreshments | ☐ material |
| ☐ lead | ☐ attend | ☐ presenter | ☐ conduct |
| ☐ projector | ☐ address | ☐ remove | ☐ expand |
| ☐ session | ☐ previous | ☐ upcoming | ☐ responsibility |

# Unit 6 Web Sites

**TOEIC では**
- 様々な「ウェブサイト」「ウェブページ」が題材として多数登場します。

**この Unit では**
- 「ウェブサイト」「ウェブページ」に関する語句･会話表現･文書などに親しみましょう。
- リスニングは「Part 3 の解き方」を学び､文法は「動詞」をもっと深く学びましょう。

## Vocabulary Attack

**1** カタカナ語になっている TOEIC 頻出語句の音声を聞いてリピートし、意味を確認しましょう。 47

| | | | |
|---|---|---|---|
| click | クリック | account | アカウント、口座 |
| log in / out | ログイン／ログアウト | link | リンク、つながり、つながる |
| sign in / out | サインイン／サインアウト | update | アップデート、更新<br>最新版・修正版にする |

**2** その他の TOEIC 頻出語句をマスターしましょう。

❶ まずは音声を聞いてリピートしましょう。 48

| | | | |
|---|---|---|---|
| form | reviewer | paperwork | post |
| consultant | laptop | approve | connection |
| social media | detail | image | complete |
| site | feature | applicant | profile |

❷ 上の表の中から、下線部に適切な英語を選び入れましょう。

| モノ | 人 | 動作 | その他 |
|---|---|---|---|
| ノート型パソコン<br>→ ________ | 応募者、申込者<br>→ ________ | 承認する<br>→ ________ | 詳細<br>→ ________ |
| 画像<br>→ ________ | 評論家、批評家<br>→ ________ | 投稿する、掲示する<br>→ ________ | 特徴、機能<br>→ ________ |
| SNS などのサービス<br>→ ________ | 相談員、顧問<br>→ ________ | 記入する、完成する<br>→ ________ | 略歴<br>→ ________ |
| 記入用紙<br>→ ________ | 場所、拠点<br>→ ________ | 書類仕事、手続き書類<br>→ ________ | 接続<br>→ ________ |

# Part 2 応答問題

**攻略ポイント** 提案・勧誘③

- WH 疑問詞や助動詞を使った「提案」「勧誘」表現が出題されます。
- これらに対する応答パターンも学び、正答率アップを狙いましょう。

**提案・勧誘の表現**

| WH 疑問詞（復習） | 助動詞 |
|---|---|
| · **Why don't you** + 動詞？<br>あなた〜したらどうですか？ / しませんか？<br>· **Why don't we** + 動詞？ 一緒に〜しませんか？<br>· **How (What) about** + 名詞 / 動名詞〜 ing?<br>〜したらどうですか？ / しませんか？ | · **Would you like** + 名詞？<br>〜はいかがですか？<br>· **Would you like to** + 動詞？<br>〜しませんか？<br>※「〜がほしいですか？」「〜したいですか？」という意味もある。 |

## Practice 1

**Step 1** 問いかけを聞いて、意味に○をつけましょう。 49

1. 提案・勧誘 / それ以外
2. 提案・勧誘 / それ以外
3. 提案・勧誘 / それ以外
4. 提案・勧誘 / それ以外
5. 提案・勧誘 / それ以外
6. 提案・勧誘 / それ以外

**Step 2** 同じ英文を聞いて、空所を埋めましょう。 49

1. (    ) (    ) the library Web site been (    )?
2. (    ) (    ) (    ) to change your (    ) name?
3. (    ) (    ) (    ) you update your (    ) page?
4. (    ) (    ) (    ) (    ) the application form online?
5. (    ) (    ) (    ) the Internet café downstairs?
6. (    ) (    ) (    ) your (    ) to download some documents?

## Practice 2

TOEIC 形式（Part 2）の問題を解きましょう。 50-52

**Step 1** 正解を選びましょう。 **Step 2** 聞き取れた単語をメモしましょう。

1. Ⓐ Ⓑ Ⓒ
2. Ⓐ Ⓑ Ⓒ
3. Ⓐ Ⓑ Ⓒ

# Part 3 会話問題

**攻略ポイント** 長文リスニング問題の基本①

- 30 ～ 40 秒間の会話を聞いて、問題に答えるのが Part 3 です。
- 会話の全てを聞き取る必要はありません。聞き取るべき情報は、設問で指定されています。
- 聞き取った内容と一致するものを選択肢から選ぶ ⇒ 聞く力だけでなく読む力も必要です。

## Part 3（会話問題）の流れを確認しましょう

### Pre-listening（会話を聞く前の準備）

☑ ① 設問 3 つを 10 秒程度で読み、どんな情報を聞き取るべきかを把握する。

**32.** Where does the **conversation most likely** take place?

どこでこの（　　　　）は（　　　　）行われている？

(A) At a station　(C) At a hotel
(B) At a post office　(D) At a fitness center

**33.** What is the woman **purchasing**?

女性は何を（　　　　）いるところ？

(A) A stamp　(C) A ticket
(B) A souvenir　(D) A video

**34.** What will **the speakers** do next?

（　　　　）は次に何をする？

(A) Visit a Web site　(C) Go downstairs
(B) Call a business　(D) Find empty seats

☑ ② 会話が始まる前に、1 問目（No. 32）の選択肢に目線を置いてスタンバイ。

### While-listening（会話を聞いている間）

☑ ③ 選択肢を見ながら会話を聞き、聞こえてきた単語や表現と一致する選択肢を選ぶ。

☑ ④ 会話の進行とともに 1 問目⇒ 2 問目⇒ 3 問目の選択肢へと目を動かす。

★30～40 秒間の会話は、およそ 3 分の 1 経過するごとに、問題を解くためのヒントが聞こえてくる。

☑ ⑤ 答えがわかっても、まだマークシートにはマークせず、目線は問題から外さない。

### Post-listening（会話を聞き終えた後）

☑ ⑥「No. 32 Where does ...」と設問の読み上げが始まったら、マークシートを塗る。

☑ ⑦ わからなければどれをマークしても OK。迷っているヒマはない。

☑ ⑧ 3 問目の設問読み上げ（No. 34　What will...）が始まったら、次の 3 問に進む（↑①に戻る）

このように 30 ～ 40 秒の会話を全て聞き取ってから問題を解くのではなく、聞きながら重要な情報をキャッチするのが重要。

# Practice 3

前ページで確認した「流れ」を意識して、Part 3 を２セット連続で解いてみましょう。 53-54

今回は、設問に和訳を付けています。事前に目を通しておきましょう。

1. What is the man looking for? 男性は何を探している？
   (A) Coffee beans
   (B) A document
   (C) An elevator
   (D) A copy machine

2. According to the woman, where can the man find an order form? 女性によると、男性はどこで注文フォームを見つけることができる？
   (A) In a storeroom
   (B) On a Web site
   (C) In the hallway
   (D) On his desk

3. Where did the man work before? どこで男性は前に働いていた？
   (A) In Chicago
   (B) In Los Angeles
   (C) In Miami
   (D) In Boston

---

55-56

4. Where is the man? どこに男性はいる？
   (A) At a bank
   (B) At a station
   (C) At a telephone company
   (D) At a store

5. Who is the man visiting in California? 男性は誰を訪ねている、カリフォルニアで？
   (A) A client
   (B) A friend
   (C) A manager
   (D) A doctor

6. What will the woman most likely ask the man? 女性はおそらく何を男性に尋ねる？
   (A) Directions to his office
   (B) Secret questions
   (C) His business number
   (D) His Log-in information

| No. | A B C D |
|---|---|
| 1 | Ⓐ Ⓑ Ⓒ Ⓓ |
| 2 | Ⓐ Ⓑ Ⓒ Ⓓ |
| 3 | Ⓐ Ⓑ Ⓒ Ⓓ |
| 4 | Ⓐ Ⓑ Ⓒ Ⓓ |
| 5 | Ⓐ Ⓑ Ⓒ Ⓓ |
| 6 | Ⓐ Ⓑ Ⓒ Ⓓ |

答え合わせの前に、
①前ページで、①～⑧の手順どおりにできたかチェック。
②次ページで、重要箇所のディクテーションに挑戦。

# Practice 4

各設問を解く上で重要な部分を再度聞いてディクテーションに挑戦し、和訳を完成させましょう。 A 57-62

**【No. 1】**

Can you tell me (　　　) the (　　　) (　　　　　　) is?

(　　　　　　　) があるか教えてくれませんか？

**【No. 2】**

There is an online (　　　　　) (　　　) on our internal (　　　) (　　　).

社内 (　　　　　) にオンライン (　　　　　) がありますよ。

**【No. 3】**

I just (　　　　　) from the (　　　　　) office.

私は、(　　　　　) オフィスから (　　　) ところなんです。

**【No. 4】**

I'm at the Bates and Norton (　　　　　　) (　　　) right now.

私は今、Bates and Norton (　　　　　) にいます。

**【No. 5】**

I'm on a business (　　　), visiting a (　　　) (　　　　　　).

私は (　　　　　　　) を訪問するのに、(　　　) 中なんです。

**【No. 6】**

If you'll answer a few (　　　　　) (　　　　　　　) for me, (以下略)

もしいくつかの (　　　　　　　　) に答えていただければ、(以下略)

前ページに戻って、答え合わせをしましょう。

# Part 5 短文穴埋め問題

**攻略ポイント** 動詞③数

- 選択肢に、「動詞」が様々な形で並んでいたら「動詞の用法」を問う問題です。
- 主語と述語の「数の一致」も頻出項目です。しっかり出題ポイントを押さえましょう。

## 文法ポイント 動詞の「数」

- **名詞**の語尾に「-s」を付けるのは、**複数形**のとき（例外：不可算名詞、不規則変化）
- 主語が**三**人称**単**数で、かつ時制が「**現**在形」のときは、**述語動詞**の語尾に「**-s**」を付ける
  ⇒**三単現の s**　例 I own a car. ⇒ He own**s** a car. / The company own**s** a car.
- 現在完了形（have+ 過去分詞）の場合も、三単現では have の代わりに **has** を使う
  例 We have heard the news. ⇒ She **has** heard the news.
- be 動詞の場合、三単現では **is / was** を使う　例 They were big. ⇒ It **was** big.
- 気をつけたい「数」の要注意ポイント：該当するほうに○を付けましょう。

| 主語 | 述語動詞 |
|---|---|
| Everybody (Everyone) | 語尾に s を【付ける・付けない】 |
| Each member | 語尾に s を【付ける・付けない】 |
| One of the customers | 語尾に s を【付ける・付けない】 |
| 不可算名詞（equipment や furniture など） | 語尾に s を【付ける・付けない】 |
| The ABC Corporation | 語尾に s を【付ける・付けない】 |
| Product reviews | 語尾に s を【付ける・付けない】 |
| The participants in the seminar | 語尾に s を【付ける・付けない】 |

ヒント まずは以下のルールに従って考えましょう。
主語に「-s」**あり** ⇒ 述語に「-s」を付けない（**なし**）　主語に「-s」**なし** ⇒ 述語に「-s」を付ける（**あり**）

## Practice 5

「語尾の特徴」を参考に、次の A ～ D の語の中から**名詞 / 動詞 / 形容詞 / 副詞**を選び、[ ] に**名 / 動 / 形 / 副**と記入しましょう。

| | A | B | C | D |
|---|---|---|---|---|
| 1 | [ ] additional | [ ] addition | [ ] add | [ ] additionally |
| 2 | [ ] preparatory | [ ] preparation | [ ] prepare | [ ] prepares |
| 3 | [ ] collection | [ ] collective | [ ] collect | [ ] collectively |
| 4 | [ ] respect | [ ] respects | [ ] respective | [ ] respectful |

## Practice 6

Practice 5 の単語から、以下の英文に合うものを選び、適切な形に変えて（　　）に記入しましょう。
※時制・態に加え「数」も意識して、正しい形で入れましょう。

1. The chef (　　　　　　) the food carefully and served it to the guests immediately.
   準備する
2. Even now, every employee deeply (　　　　　　　　　) the company founder, Ms. Collins.
   尊敬する
3. Unused office equipment (　　　　　　　　　) by a charity group next Monday.
   回収する
4. Your name (　　　　　　) to the mailing list when we received your first order.
   加える

## Practice 7

TOEIC 形式（Part 5）の問題です。空欄に入る適切な語を (A) ~ (D) から選びましょう。

解答時間：1 分 30 秒

1. One of our consultants ------- a Web meeting with the CEO of a Chinese IT company.
   (A) arrange
   (B) arranging
   (C) arranged
   (D) is arranged

2. The details of the online conference ------- three days before the scheduled date.
   (A) announce
   (B) announcing
   (C) announces
   (D) were announced

3. Ms. Cho from Human Resources ------- summer interns through online tutorials.
   (A) train
   (B) will be trained
   (C) training
   (D) trains

# Part 7　読解問題

**攻略ポイント**　フォーム・定型用紙

- アンケートや申込書などが多い。まずは内容を確認しましょう。
- 「表形式」の場合は、項目が何を示しているかもチェックしましょう。
- 日本では「○」と「×」を使い分けますが、英語圏では「×」も「該当する」の意味です。

オンラインフォームを読みましょう。

http://happyhomeSS.com

## Happy Home Garden and Yard Super Stores

How satisfied are you with your garden product purchase? Please click on the appropriate boxes to indicate your responses.

(1 = Completely unsatisfied, 2 = Somewhat unsatisfied, 3 = No opinion,
4 = Somewhat satisfied, 5 = Completely satisfied)

**Customer Name:** Mary Plum

| Satisfaction score: | 1 | 2 | 3 | 4 | 5 |
|---|---|---|---|---|---|
| **Product quality:** Were the products made well? Did they meet expectations? | | | × | | |
| **Delivery service:** Was delivery on time? Were delivery staff courteous? | × | | | | |
| **After sale service:** Did after-sale service meet your expectations? | | | | × | |

**サンプル設問**　①まずは設問の意味を確認し、②文書からそれらの情報を探しましょう。

1. Who **most likely** is Mary Plum?
    (A) A shopper
    (B) A store clerk
    (C) A tourist
    (D) A passenger

**設問の意味**
Mary Plum とは（　　　　　）誰？

**ヒント** Mary Plum の名前を探そう。
⇒更に、このフォームはどんな人が書くものか探ってみよう。

2. **According to** the survey, what is Mary Plum most satisfied with?
    (A) The quality of the products
    (B) The service after the purchase
    (C) The prices of the products
    (D) The delivery options available

**設問の意味**
このアンケート（　　　　　）Mary Plum が最も満足しているのは何？

**ヒント** most satisfied を表す数字は「1～5」のどれ？

# Practice 8

読解問題に挑戦しましょう。

**解き方の手順**

1. まずは文書の種類を確認しましょう。 Web page ⇒ ウェブサイト上の1ページ
2. 続いて設問を読んで「何を答えないといけないか」チェックしましょう。
3. 本文だけではなく文書の隅々にまで目を向けましょう。

Questions 3-4 refer to the following Web page. 解答時間：2分

http://macksbike.co.ca/products

## Mack's Bike Shop

We have a wide range of models, accessories and services. First, click on the general type of bicycle you need. Then, click NEXT to explore more.

**What kind of bike do you need?**

○ **Grocery Getters**
Most affordable bicycles for shopping, carrying and pleasure. You can choose from one-speed and three-speed models.

○ **Commuting Bikes**
High-end bicycles perfect for heavy city use in all kinds of weather.

○ **Off-Road Bikes**
Sturdy frames and fat tires make these bikes the best for dirt roads and mountain trails.

(Note: Battery power options are only available for specified models.)

NEXT

3. Why should someone click "NEXT"?
   (A) To learn how to ride a bike
   (B) To sell a second-hand bike
   (C) To see a list of bicycles
   (D) To choose a payment method

4. What is indicated about Mack's Bike Shop?
   (A) They offer discounts to students.
   (B) They ship products internationally.
   (C) Some of their models can be battery-powered.
   (D) Some of their models are hand-made.

答え合わせの前に、次のページで精読をしましょう！

## 精読タイム！

1語1語に注目しながら、正確に和訳しましょう。

### 設問の精読

3. Why **should** someone **click** "NEXT"?
   なぜ「NEXT」を（　　　　　　　　）？

4. What **is indicated** about Mack's Bike Shop?
   Mack 自転車店について何と（　　　　　　　　）？

### 文書の精読　★重要な部分だけ！

First, click on the **general** type of bicycle you need.
まずはあなたが希望する自転車の（　　　　　　）タイプをクリックしてください。

Then click NEXT to **explore** more.
その後で、NEXT を押してください、もっと詳しく（　　　　　　）ために。

**Battery power** options are only **available** for specified models.
（　　　　　　　）オプションは、特定の製品にのみ（　　　　　　）。

### 選択肢の精読　★重要な部分だけ！

3. (A) To learn **how to ride** a bike　自転車の（　　　　　　　）を学ぶため
   (B) To sell a **second-hand** bike（　　　　　　　）自転車を売るため

4. (B) They **ship** products internationally.　海外へ製品を（　　　　　　　）。
   (C) Some of their models can be **battery powered**.
   一部の製品は（　　　　　　　）にできる。
   (D) Some of their models are **hand-made**.　一部の製品は（　　　　　）である。

# Reflection

Unit 6 で学んだ単語・表現をチェックしましょう。　意味がすぐに浮かぶようになるまで、反復練習しましょう。

- ☐ form
- ☐ consultant
- ☐ social media
- ☐ site
- ☐ Would you like
- ☐ look for
- ☐ reviewer
- ☐ laptop
- ☐ detail
- ☐ feature
- ☐ most likely
- ☐ prepare
- ☐ paperwork
- ☐ approve
- ☐ image
- ☐ applicant
- ☐ conversation
- ☐ respect
- ☐ post
- ☐ connection
- ☐ complete
- ☐ profile
- ☐ speaker
- ☐ explore

# Unit 7 Advertising

TOEIC では
• 様々な「宣伝」「広告」が題材として多数登場します。

この Unit では
• 「宣伝・広告」に関する語句・会話表現・文書などに親しみましょう。
• リスニングは「Part 4 の解き方」、文法は「代名詞」を学びましょう。

## Vocabulary Attack

**1** カタカナ語になっている TOEIC 頻出語句の音声を聞いてリピートし、意味を確認しましょう。 A 63

| | | | |
|---|---|---|---|
| catalog | カタログ | bargain | お買い得品、掘り出し物 |
| delivery | 配達 | receipt | レシート、領収書 |
| promotion (promo) | 広報宣伝、販売促進 | customize | 特注する、要望に合わせて作る |

**2** その他の TOEIC 頻出語句をマスターしましょう。

❶ まずは音声を聞いてリピートしましょう。 A 64

| | | | |
|---|---|---|---|
| demonstrate | complimentary | exchange | look for |
| stop by | shipment | available | brochure |
| cover | advertisement | specialize | refund |
| fee | guarantee | flyer | voucher |

❷ 上の表の中から、下線部に適切な英語を選び入れましょう。

**モノ**

チラシ
→ ________________

広告
→ ________________

割引券、引換券
→ ________________

パンフレット
→ ________________

**動作**

探す
→ ________________

交換（する）
→ ________________

実演する
→ ________________

返金（する）
→ ________________

特化する
→ ________________

保証（する）
→ ________________

～を含む、～に及ぶ
→ ________________

立ち寄る
→ ________________

**その他**

無料の
→ ________________

発送、出荷
→ ________________

入手・使用できる
→ ________________

料金
→ ________________

# Part 2 応答問題

**攻略ポイント** 申し出など

- 「**私が**〜しましょうか？」「**一緒に**〜しませんか？」などの「申し出・提案」表現に注意しましょう。
- 疑問文とは答え方が違うので、その点にも気を付けることが重要です。

**申し出・提案の表現**

**WH 疑問詞**
・**Why don't I** + 動詞？ 私が〜しましょうか？

**助動詞**
・**Shall I** + 動詞？ 私が〜しましょうか？
・**Shall we** + 動詞？ 一緒に〜しませんか？

【復習】・**Why don't we** + 動詞？ 一緒に〜しませんか？
・**How (What) about** + 名詞 / 動名詞〜 ing? 〜したらどうですか？ / 〜しませんか？

## Practice 1

**Step 1** 問いかけを聞いて、意味に○をつけましょう。 65

1. 申し出・提案 / それ以外
2. 申し出・提案 / それ以外
3. 申し出・提案 / それ以外
4. 申し出・提案 / それ以外
5. 申し出・提案 / それ以外
6. 申し出・提案 / それ以外

**Step 2** 同じ英文を聞いて、空所を埋めましょう。 65

1. ( ) in charge of the ( ) campaign?
2. ( ) ( ) give you a quick ( )?
3. ( ) ( ) you find that free ( ) ( )?
4. ( ) ( ) ( ) show you our online catalog?
5. ( ) ( ) get a ( ) without a ( )?
6. ( ) ( ) placing an ( ) in a local paper?

## Practice 2

TOEIC 形式（Part 2）の問題を解きましょう。 66-68

**Step 1** 正解を選びましょう。 **Step 2** 聞き取れた単語をメモしましょう。

1. Ⓐ Ⓑ Ⓒ
2. Ⓐ Ⓑ Ⓒ
3. Ⓐ Ⓑ Ⓒ

# Part 4　トーク問題

**攻略ポイント**　**長文リスニング問題の基本②**

- 30～40秒間のトークを聞いて、問題に答えるのがPart 4です。
- Part 3と異なり、話者1人のトークは切れ目なく続きますが、おおよそ3分の1経過するごとに、目線を次の設問に移動させながら聞くことが重要です。

## Part 4の流れを確認しよう

### Pre-listening（トークを聞く前の準備）

☑ ① 設問3つを10秒程度で読み、どんな情報を聞き取るべきかを把握する。

71. What is being **advertised**?　何が（　　　）されている？

(A) A business hotel　(C) A business course
(B) A package tour　(D) A food item

72. Who **most likely** are **the listeners**?（　　　）は（　　　）誰？

(A) Hotel staff　(C) College students
(B) Air passengers　(D) Grocery shoppers

73. What does **the speaker** ask about?（　　　）は何について尋ねている？

(A) A payment method　(C) A money-back guarantee
(B) Seat options　(D) Special rates

☑ ② トークが始まる前に、1問目（No. 71）の選択肢に目線を置いてスタンバイ。

### While-listening（トークを聞いている間）

☑ ③ 選択肢を見ながらとトークを聞き、聞こえてきた単語や表現と一致する選択肢を選ぶ。
☑ ④ トークの進行とともに1問目⇒2問目⇒3問目の選択肢へと目を動かす。

★ 30～40秒間のトークは、およそ3分の1経過するごとに、問題を解くためのヒントが聞こえてくる。

☑ ⑤ 答えがわかっても、まだマークシートにはマークせず、目線は問題から外さない。

### Post-listening（トークを聞き終えた後）

☑ ⑥「No. 71　What is ...」と設問の読み上げが始まったら、マークシートを塗る。
☑ ⑦ わからなければどれをマークしてもOK。迷っているヒマはない。
☑ ⑧ 3問目の設問読み上げ（No. 73　What ...）が始まったら、次の3問に進む（↑①に戻る）。

このように30～40秒のトークを全て聞き取ってから問題を解くのではなく、聞きながら重要な情報をキャッチするのが重要。

# Practice 3

前ページで確認した「流れ」を意識して、Part 4 を2セット連続で解いてみましょう。 69-70

今回は、設問の一部に和訳を付けています。事前に目を通しておきましょう。

1. What is **being advertised**? 何が（ ? ）
   (A) Security systems
   (B) Financial services
   (C) Cars
   (D) Homes

2. When did Briar Brothers start its business? Briar Brothers はいつ事業を始めた？
   (A) 20 years ago
   (B) 50 years ago
   (C) More than 100 years ago
   (D) More than 200 years ago

3. What does Briar Brothers provide for free? Briar Brothers は何を無料で提供している？
   (A) Professional consultation
   (B) Price estimates
   (C) Life insurance
   (D) Bank accounts

---

71-72

4. Where would the announcement most likely be heard? どこでこのお知らせはおそらく聞かれている？
   (A) On television
   (B) In an airport
   (C) At a sports stadium
   (D) In a department store

5. What items **are sold at a 70 percent discount**? どの製品が（ ? ）
   (A) Home accessories
   (B) Cosmetics
   (C) Clothing
   (D) Fashion magazines

6. Where **can furniture be found**? どこで（ ? ）
   (A) On the 1st floor
   (B) On the 2nd floor
   (C) On the 3rd floor
   (D) On the 4th floor

答え合わせの前に、
(1) 前ページで、①～⑧の手順どおりにできたかチェック。
(2) 次ページで、重要箇所のディクテーションに挑戦。

| No. | A B C D |
|---|---|
| 1 | Ⓐ Ⓑ Ⓒ Ⓓ |
| 2 | Ⓐ Ⓑ Ⓒ Ⓓ |
| 3 | Ⓐ Ⓑ Ⓒ Ⓓ |
| 4 | Ⓐ Ⓑ Ⓒ Ⓓ |
| 5 | Ⓐ Ⓑ Ⓒ Ⓓ |
| 6 | Ⓐ Ⓑ Ⓒ Ⓓ |

## Practice 4

各設問を解く上で重要な部分を再度聞いてディクテーションに挑戦し、和訳を完成させましょう。 A 73-78

**【No. 1】**

Briar Brothers (　　　　) (　　　　) will help you find the answers to tough questions like these.

Briar Brothers (　　　　　　) は、答えを探すお手伝いをいたします、このような難しい問いへの。

**【No. 2】**

For over (　　　　　　), Briar Brothers has been providing expert (　　　　) on personal (　　　　　).

(　　　　) 以上にわたって、Briar Brothers は提供してきました、個人 (　　　　) に関する専門的 (　　　　) を。

**【No. 3】**

Visit our Web site to book a (　　　　) (　　　　) (　　　　　　) at a location near you.

当社のウェブサイトをご訪問ください、(　　　　　　　) をご予約いただくには、お近くの拠点で。

**【No.4】**

Welcome to Rayworth (　　　　　　) (　　　　).

Rayworth (　　　　) へようこそ。

**【No. 5】**

And save up to 70% on specially marked (　　　　) (　　　　).

特別な印のついた (　　　　　) では、最大70%節約できます (＝値引きになっています)。

**【No. 6】**

Check out the (　　　　)-off sale on our superb selection of furniture and home accessories in the Beautiful Home Zone on the (　　　　) floor.

(　　　　　) セールをチェックしてください、家具と家庭用装飾品の素晴らしい品ぞろえに対する (　　　　　) 階の「美しい家ゾーン」で。

前ページに戻って、答え合わせをましょう。

# Part 5　短文穴埋め問題

**攻略ポイント**　代名詞

- 選択肢に代名詞が並んでいたら、ここで学ぶ項目を意識して解きましょう。
- 人称代名詞は「数」「性別」「用法」の３点に注意しましょう。

## 文法ポイント　代名詞

- 名詞の代わりとして用いられる語　例 Mr. Kato ⇒ **he**/ABC, Inc. ⇒ **it**
  ⇒名詞と同じように、主語、目的語、補語になり、前置詞の後ろにも置かれる。
- 「人称代名詞」:主格、目的格、所有格、独立所有格（＝所有代名詞）、再帰代名詞など、使う場面によって形が変化する（＝格変化）。
- 人称代名詞の一覧：空所を埋めて完成させましょう。

| | 主格<br>～は | 所有格<br>～の | 目的格<br>～を・に | 独立所有格<br>～のもの | 再帰代名詞<br>～自身 |
|---|---|---|---|---|---|
| 私 | I | | me | mine | myself |
| あなた | | | you | your**s** | yourself |
| 彼 | | his | | his | |
| 彼女 | | her | | her**s** | herself |
| それ | | | it | its | itself |
| 私たち | | | us | our**s** | ourselves |
| あなたたち | | your | | your**s** | |
| 彼（女）ら・それら | | | them | their**s** | themselves |

- 主な用法

主格 主語になる　例 **She** has a receipt. / **It** opens at noon.
所有格 名詞の前に置かれる　例 This is **his** car. / The store changed **its** policy.
目的格 動詞や前置詞の目的語になる　例 Liz called **him**.　例 in front of **them**

**所有格か独立所有格か迷ったら：**（以下の二択問題に挑戦してみましょう）
後ろに名詞が　⇒ 所有格　例 I drove [ her / hers ] car, and she drove [my / mine ].
後ろに own が ⇒ 所有格　例 I drove [ my / mine ] own (car).

**再帰代名詞の強調用法**：意味を強めるだけなので、これがなくても文意は変わらない。
例 Ms. Patel reserved a room **herself**.
Patel さんは**自分で**部屋を予約した。

## Practice 5

数、性別、用法に気を付けて、(　　) に正しい代名詞を入れ、さらに太字の部分の意味を記入しましょう。

1. Ms. Evans thanked (　　　　) **colleagues** for being helpful in drawing up the sales plan.
   意味：

2. These two smartphones look similar, but (　　　　) are **functionally** different.
   意味：

3. The Beatrix art museum will open (　　　　) doors to the public **in two weeks**.
   意味：

4. The chef **prepared** the food carefully and served (　　　　) to the guests.
   意味：

## Practice 6

TOEIC 形式（Part 5）の問題です。空欄に入る適切な語を (A) ~ (D) から選びましょう。

解答時間：1 分 30 秒

1. Employees must wear ------- ID badges at all times while on company premises.
   (A) they
   (B) their
   (C) theirs
   (D) them

2. Complimentary shipping attracted more online shoppers than ------- expected.
   (A) we
   (B) our
   (C) us
   (D) ourselves

3. Ms. Philips, the owner of the Rooftop Café, makes it a point to design all the flyers -------.
   (A) her
   (B) him
   (C) himself
   (D) herself

# Part 7 読解問題

**攻略ポイント** **広告文**

- アピールしたいポイント（何？どこ？いつ？など）は目立つように書かれています。
- 重要だけどアピールしたくないポイント（適用条件、除外品など）は小さく目立たないように書かれていることもあります。
- もっと情報がほしくなったときの入手方法や連絡方法も書かれていることが多くあります。

広告文を読みましょう。

## Ansonberry Park Summer Weekend Art Fair

9:00 a.m. to 9:00 p.m. every Saturday and Sunday
June 4 to September 4

Enjoy a day in the park, and enrich your life with a wide variety of artwork. Connect with more than 100 local artists offering their works directly to you. Get great prices on paintings, photographs, ceramic crafts, sculptures, jewelry, glass art, and much, much more!

Visit www.ansonparkartfair.com for details.

**サンプル設問** ①まずは設問の意味を確認し、②文書からそれらの情報を探しましょう。

1. What **is indicated** about the art fair?
   (A) International foods are served.
   (B) Guided tours are available.
   (C) Children can visit for free.
   (D) It includes a wide variety of art.

**設問の意味**
アート祭りについて何が（　　　　）？

**ヒント** この広告全体が「art fair」に関することなので、選択肢と見比べながら、1つ1つ消し込んでいく必要がある。

2. What can **visitors** do at the fair?
   (A) Learn watercolor painting
   (B) Enter museums for free.
   (C) Design their own jewelry
   (D) Purchase art from local artists

**設問の意味**
このお祭りで、(　　　　) は何ができる?

**ヒント** 「お祭りで**できること**」に絞って情報収集しよう。

## Practice 7

読解問題に挑戦しましょう。

**解き方の手順**

1. まずは文書の種類を確認しましょう。 advertisement ⇒ 広告文
2. 続いて設問を読んで「何を答えないといけないか」チェックしましょう。
3. 本文だけではなく文書の隅々にまで目を向けましょう。

Questions 3-4 refer to the following advertisement. 解答時間：2分

**Max Biz Office Supply Super Store**

All you need for your office, and more!

Sign up for our printer ink cartridge subscription service with free delivery!

For in-store shoppers, this week's special deals include:
—**Taylor's Fine Copy Paper:** 500-sheet pack $5.25 (Box of 10 packs: $50.00)
—**Rechargeable batteries:** all major brands and sizes, 20% off manufacturer's price

**Copy & Printing**

Our Copy & Printing Center offers professional duplication and printing services. From business cards to large signs. We've got you covered.

To order copies or printing online, or to browse our online catalogue, go to MaxBizOfficeSupplies.com.

3. What is indicated about the subscription service?
   (A) It is available only to store members.
   (B) It covers both copy paper and batteries.
   (C) Free delivery is included.
   (D) The subscription fee is $5.25.

4. What can a customer do online?
   (A) Order a printing job
   (B) Get a 20% discount on copy paper
   (C) Customize a catalogue
   (D) Hire temporary office staff

答え合わせの前に、次のページで精読をしましょう！

## 精読タイム！

1語1語に注目しながら、正確に和訳しましょう。

### 設問の精読

3. What **is indicated** about the subscription service?
定期購買サービスについて何が（　　　　　　　　　　　　　　　　　　）？

4. What **can a customer do** online?
（　　　　　）はオンラインで何を（　　　　　　　　　　　　　）？

### 文書の精読 ★重要な部分だけ！

**Sign up for** our printer ink cartridge subscription service with **free delivery**!
（　　　　　　　　　）、（　　　　　　　　　　　　）付きの当社のプリンターインクカートリッジの定期購買サービスに。

To **order** copies or printing online, or to **browse** our online catalogue,
コピーや印刷をオンラインで（　　　　　　）には、もしくはオンラインのカタログを（　　　　　　）には、
go to MaxBizOfficeSupplies.com.
MaxBizOfficeSupplies.com にお進みください。

### 選択肢の精読 ★重要な部分だけ！

3. (A) It is **available** only to store members. ストア会員だけ（　　　　　　　）。
(B) It covers both copy paper and **batteries**. コピー用紙と（　　　　　　　）も対象に入る。
(C) Free delivery **is included**. 無料配達が（　　　　　　　）。

4. (A) Order a printing **job** 印刷（　　　　　　　）を注文する
(C) **Customize** a catalogue カタログを（　　　　　　　）
(D) **Hire** temporary office staff 臨時のオフィススタッフを（　　　　　　　）

## Reflection

Unit 7 で学んだ単語・表現をチェックしましょう。 意味がすぐに浮かぶようになるまで、反復練習しましょう。

| | | | |
|---|---|---|---|
| ☐ delivery | ☐ promotion | ☐ receipt | ☐ customize |
| ☐ demonstrate | ☐ complimentary | ☐ exchange | ☐ look for |
| ☐ stop by | ☐ shipment | ☐ available | ☐ brochure |
| ☐ cover | ☐ advertisement (ad) | ☐ specialize | ☐ refund |
| ☐ fee | ☐ purchase | ☐ flyer | ☐ voucher |
| ☐ financial | ☐ clothing | ☐ artwork | ☐ accessory |

# Unit 8 Information Technology

TOEIC では ▸ • 様々な「情報技術(ハードウェア、ソフトウェア、通信)」が題材として多数登場します。

この Unit では ▸ • 「IT」に関する語句・会話表現・文書などに親しみましょう。
• 文法は「関係代名詞」を学びましょう。

## Vocabulary Attack

**1** カタカナ語になっている TOEIC 頻出語句の音声を聞いてリピートし、意味を確認しましょう。 A 79

| | | | |
|---|---|---|---|
| cable | ケーブル(TV)、大綱、電線 | tablet | タブレット端末 |
| Internet | インターネット | program | コンピュータプログラム、ソフト |
| app | ソフトウェア、アプリ | data | データ |

**2** その他の TOEIC 頻出語句をマスターしましょう。

❶ まずは音声を聞いてリピートしましょう。 A 80

| | | | |
|---|---|---|---|
| video | save | security | develop |
| upgrade | terminal | search | work station |
| subscription | text | function | e-reader |
| delete | budget | contract | confidential |

❷ 上の表の中から、下線部に適切な英語を選び入れましょう。

**モノ**

電子書籍リーダー
→ ________________

動画、映像
→ ________________

高性能コンピュータ
→ ________________

端末機器(パソコンなど)
→ ________________

**動作**

削除する
→ ________________

機能(する)
→ ________________

開発する
→ ________________

性能改善(する)
→ ________________

保存する
→ ________________

検索(する)
→ ________________

テキストメッセージ(を送る)
→ ________________________

**その他**

予算
→ ________________

契約(書)
→ ________________

定期利用契約
→ ________________

極秘の
→ ________________

安全、警備
→ ________________

# Parts 3 & 4 会話問題＆トーク問題

**攻略ポイント** 場面が社内の場合

- 同僚との話に出てくる話題や単語を押さえましょう。
- 同僚だからこそ「話を割愛・省略」する部分などにも要注意です。
- 解く手順は、Unit 6 ～ 7 で紹介済みです。忘れないよう定期的に見直しておきましょう。

## 社内での会話・トークの聞き取りポイント

- 知り合い同士 ⇒ いきなり本題に入ることが多い。
- 知らない者同士 ⇒ 自己紹介は簡潔。氏名＋部署名のみ伝えるパターンが多い。

**主な部署名**

| | | | |
|---|---|---|---|
| 営業 | □ sales | 広報 | □ public relations |
| 経理 | □ accounting | 警備 | □ security |
| 人事 | □ personnel | 技術サポート | □ technical support |
| | □ human resources | | □ tech support |

- 主な内容

**説明・案内** 仕事やプライベートについて説明や案内をする。

例 We are having a visitor from the headquarters this afternoon.

**提案・勧誘・依頼** 仕事やプライベートの計画に関する提案・勧誘・依頼をする。

例 How about going to that new Italian restaurant?

**課題解決** 課題や問題点を述べた上で、解決策を模索する。

例 I couldn't attend the training session. What should I do?

- 話の終盤に注意：終盤になんらかのアクションをしたり、頼んだりすることが多い。

**どんなアクション？**

| | | | |
|---|---|---|---|
| 連絡する | □ contact | 確認する | □ confirm |
| チェックする | □ review | 修正する | □ revise |
| | □ check | | □ update |
| 提出する | □ submit | 掲示・掲載する | □ post |
| 配る | □ distribute | コピーする | □ copy |
| | □ pass around | | □ make photocopies |

## Practice 1

Part 3 ⇒ Part 4 を 1 セットずつ連続で解いてみましょう。

81-82

事前に「設問」に目を通しておくことが重要(一部にのみ和訳を付けています)。

1. Who most likely is the woman?
   - (A) An art collector
   - (B) A new employee
   - (C) A security guard
   - (D) A sales representative

2. What is the woman pleased with?　女性は何に対して喜んでいる？
   - (A) Her computer screen
   - (B) The man's design
   - (C) Her job contract
   - (D) The Internet connection

3. What will probably happen next?
   - (A) A product demonstration
   - (B) A job interview
   - (C) Office relocation
   - (D) Introduction to colleagues

---

83-84

4. On what day does the talk take place?
   - (A) Friday
   - (B) Saturday
   - (C) Sunday
   - (D) Monday

5. What will the speaker and the listeners work on?　話し手と聞き手は何に取り組む予定？
   - (A) Security checks
   - (B) TV advertisements
   - (C) Traffic signs
   - (D) Children's toys

6. What is Maria ready to provide?
   - (A) The project budget
   - (B) The yearly schedule
   - (C) IT assistance
   - (D) A video game

答え合わせの前に、次でディクテーションをしましょう！

| No. | A | B | C | D |
|---|---|---|---|---|
| 1 | Ⓐ | Ⓑ | Ⓒ | Ⓓ |
| 2 | Ⓐ | Ⓑ | Ⓒ | Ⓓ |
| 3 | Ⓐ | Ⓑ | Ⓒ | Ⓓ |
| 4 | Ⓐ | Ⓑ | Ⓒ | Ⓓ |
| 5 | Ⓐ | Ⓑ | Ⓒ | Ⓓ |
| 6 | Ⓐ | Ⓑ | Ⓒ | Ⓓ |

## Practice 2

各設問を解く上で重要な部分を再度聞いてディクテーションに挑戦し、和訳を完成させましょう。 A 85-90

**【No. 1】**

( ) to Orris Media Production, Linda.
Orris Media Production 社へ（ ）、Linda。

I work in Human Resources, and help the ( ) ( ) settle in.
私は人事部で働いていて、（ ）が落ち着くのを手伝っています。

**【No. 2】**

I really like this ( ) ( ).
この（ ）がとても気に入っています。

**【No. 3】**

I'll sometimes be working with an animation ( ), but
私は、ときどき、アニメーション（ ）とも一緒に作業するようですが、

I still ( ) ( ) any of them.
まだ誰とも（ ）。

Let's go over, and I'll ( ) you to them.
さあ行きましょう、私があなたを彼らに（ ）。

**【No. 4】**

Thank you all for coming to ( ) today.
皆さん、今日は（ ）来てくれてありがとう。

I know that we all have other things to do on ( ).
（ ）にはみんな他にやることがあるのはわかっています。

**【No. 5】**

It's crucial that we complete the full list of ( ) ( )
私たちが（ ）の全リストを完了しておくことはきわめて重要です、

to make sure our online meeting system is absolutely ( ).
私たちのオンライン会議システムが完全に（ ）であることを確認するために。

**【No. 6】**

I've spoken to Maria in the ( ) ( ),
私は（ ）の Maria と話をしたのですが、

and she's ready to ( ) us by video conference.
彼女は私たちを（ ）準備を整えてくれています、ビデオ会議を使って。

前ページに戻って、答え合わせをしましょう。

# Part 5 短文穴埋め問題

**攻略ポイント** 関係代名詞

- 選択肢に関係代名詞が並んでいたら、ここで学ぶ項目を意識して解きましょう。
- 関係代名詞は「先行詞」と「格」の２点に注意して選びましょう。

## 文法ポイント 関係代名詞

- 代名詞である ⇒ 名詞の代わりとして用いられる。
- 節（S + V）が後ろに続く ⇒ 前の節と「連結・関連付ける」。つまり、接続詞のような働きをする。

I have met the person. She developed a gaming app.
名詞　代名詞

（私はその人物に出会った。彼女はゲームアプリを開発した）

**この２文を、関係代名詞を使って、１つにまとめると**

I have met the person **who** developed a gaming app.
先行詞　関係代名詞

関係代名詞が導く節

（私は ゲームアプリを開発した 人物に会った）

語順の違いに要注意：
英語では：　**名詞**＋［説明語句］
日本語では：［説明語句］＋**名詞**

- 関係代名詞の一覧：空所を埋めて完成させましょう。

| 先行詞の種類 | | 主格 | 所有格 | 目的格 |
|---|---|---|---|---|
| 人 | 例 client | (　　　) | whose | whom |
| モノ・動物 | 例 product | (　　　) | whose | which |
| 共通 | 例 client, product | (　　　) | なし | that |

**主格** 関係代名詞が、その後ろに続く節の主語（S）になる

例 We hired the man **who** presented at the meeting.
先行詞　(S)　(V)

**所有格** 名詞の前に置かれる

例 This is the company **whose** logo recently became very popular.
先行詞　名詞

**目的格** 後ろに続く節の動詞や前置詞の目的語（O）になる

例 The clients **whom** Liz contacted seem satisfied with her service.
先行詞　(O)　(S)　(V)

## Practice 3

先行詞の種類や格に気を付けて（　　）に正しい関係代名詞を入れ、さらに、太字の部分の意味を記入しましょう。

1. The tablets and e-readers (　　　　　　) are **displayed behind** the counter are on sale.
   意味：

2. This database is not **accessible** to those employees (　　　　　　) were just hired.
   意味：

3. The radio show will **feature** a guitarist (　　　　　　) album is on the best-seller list.
   意味：

4. The promo code (　　　　　　) we found on the **flyer** is no longer valid.
   意味：

## Practice 4

TOEIC 形式（Part 5）の問題です。空欄に入る適切な語を (A) ~ (D) から選びましょう。

解答時間：1 分 30 秒

1. The council will review the budgets ------- three Web designers have submitted online.
   (A) who
   (B) whom
   (C) whose
   (D) which

2. In this course, we learn about the artists ------- paintings mark the highest level of achievement in modern Europe.
   (A) who
   (B) whom
   (C) whose
   (D) which

3. Those ------ use this chat application are advised to download the updated version.
   (A) which
   (B) who
   (C) whose
   (D) whom

# Part 7　読解問題

**攻略ポイント**　チャット・テキストメッセージ

- スマートフォンやパソコン上でのメッセージのやりとりなので、日本語の場合と同様に、省略や会話表現の使用など、通常の文書とは異なる点に注意しましょう。
- 設問中１問は、ある特定のメッセージの「意図」を問う問題。「書き手の名前」と「送信時刻」を頼りにメッセージを探し、前後の流れからその内容を読み取りましょう。

テキストメッセージのやりとりを読みましょう。

**Albert Logan　3:08 P.M.**
Hi Kim. My team's demonstrating a new smartphone app at the staff meeting next week. Did you get my e-mail about it?

**Kimberly Mains　3:54 P.M.**
Sorry, I've been busy with accounting program updates. When is it?

**Albert Logan　3:56 P.M.**
Tuesday 3:00-4:00. You'll be there, won't you?

**Kimberly Mains　4:41 P.M.**
Sure, I think I can make it on Tuesday.

**Albert Logan　4:42 P.M.**
Thanks! Your advice and feedback will be a big help.

**サンプル設問**　①まずは設問の意味を確認し、②文書からそれらの情報を探しましょう。

**1.** What does Mr. Logan **want** Ms. Mains **to see**?

(A) His team's demonstration
(B) His search result
(C) Confidential data
(D) A cable TV program

**設問の意味**
Logan さんは Mains さんに何(　　　　　　　)?

**ヒント** Logan さんのメッセージから読み取ろう。

**2.** At 4:41 P.M., what does Ms. Mains mean when she writes, "I can make it on Tuesday"?

(A) She will call Mr. Logan on Tuesday.
(B) Her schedule is full until Tuesday.
(C) She is able to go to the meeting on Tuesday.
(D) She can finish her report by Tuesday.

**設問の意味**
午後 4:41 に Mains さんが「I can make it on Tuesday」と書いた意味は？

**ヒント** このセリフが書いてある前後の内容から読み取ろう。

## Practice 5

読解問題に挑戦しましょう。

**解き方の手順**

1. まずは文書の種類を確認しましょう。 online chat discussion ⇒ チャットのやりとり
2. 続いて設問を読んで「何を答えないといけないか」チェックしましょう。
3. 本文だけではなく文書の隅々にまで目を向けましょう。

Questions 3-4 refer to the following online chat discussion. 解答時間：2分

| | |
|---|---|
| **Lori Gates** 11:54 A.M. | Thank you for sitting in at our discussion with Alax Company yesterday. |
| **Sam Easton** 11:58 A.M. | No problem, it was my pleasure. I thought they really liked the stock management system your team developed. |
| **Lori Gates** 12:03 P.M. | Yes, but they say our monthly subscription fee is too much for their budget. |
| **Sam Easton** 12:07 P.M. | I see. I've known them for years through other projects. They're tough negotiators. |
| **Lori Gates** 12:10 P.M. | Very tough! But I feel we're close to signing a contract. Our next meeting is at their office tomorrow at 2:00 p.m. |
| **Sam Easton** 12:14 P.M. | Let me know if I can be of any help. |

**3.** What is Ms. Gates thankful for?

(A) Program updates
(B) A product review
(C) Employee training
(D) Attendance at a meeting

**4.** At 12:07 P.M., what does Mr. Easton most likely mean when he writes, "They're tough negotiators"?

(A) Alax Company is growing fast.
(B) Alax Company will demand a discount.
(C) Alax Company wants to hire him.
(D) Alax Company is a start-up company.

答え合わせの前に、次のページで精読をしましょう！

## 精読タイム！

1語1語に注目しながら、正確に和訳しましょう。

### 設問の精読

3. What is Ms. Gates **thankful** for?
Gates さんは何に対して（　　　　　　　　　　）？

4. At 12:07 P.M., what does Mr. Easton **most likely** mean when he writes, "They're tough negotiators"?
午後 12:07 に Easton さんが「They're tough negotiators」と書いたのは、（　　　　　　　　　　）どういう意味？

### 文書の精読 ★重要な部分だけ！

Thank you for **sitting in** at our discussions with Alax Company yesterday.
昨日は Alax 社との話し合いに（　　　　　　　　　　）、ありがとう。

They say our monthly subscription **fee** is too much for their **budget**.
彼らは言っているんですよ、当社の月額利用（　　　　）は彼らの（　　　　　　）には高すぎると。

I've known them **for years** through other projects.
私は、他のプロジェクトを通して彼らのことは（　　　　）知っている。

They're **tough negotiators**.
彼らは（　　　　　　　　　　）ですよ。

### 選択肢の精読 ★重要な部分だけ！

3. (A) Program **updates** プログラムの（　　　　　　）
(B) A product **review** 製品の（　　　　　　）
(D) **Attendance** at a meeting 会合への（　　　　　　）

4. (B) Alax Company **will demand** a discount. Alax 社は値引きを（　　　　　　）。
(D) Alax Company is a **start-up** company. Alax 社は（　　　　　　）会社だ。

# Reflection

Unit 8 で学んだ単語・表現をチェックしましょう。 意味がすぐに浮かぶようになるまで、反復練習しましょう。

| | | | |
|---|---|---|---|
| ☐ app | ☐ save | ☐ security | ☐ develop |
| ☐ upgrade | ☐ terminal | ☐ search | ☐ work station |
| ☐ subscription | ☐ text | ☐ function | ☐ e-reader |
| ☐ delete | ☐ budget | ☐ contract | ☐ confidential |
| ☐ introduce | ☐ take place | ☐ work on | ☐ those who |
| ☐ make it | ☐ feedback | ☐ negotiator | ☐ demand |

# Unit 9 Phone Calls

**TOEIC では**
- 「電話での会話」「留守電メッセージ」「自動録音メッセージ」などが題材として多数登場します。

**この Unit では**
- 「電話でのやりとり」に関する語句・会話表現・文書などに親しみましょう。
- 文法は「前置詞・接続詞」を学びましょう。

## Vocabulary Attack

**1** カタカナ語になっている TOEIC 頻出語句の音声を聞いてリピートし、意味を確認しましょう。 B 02

| | | | |
|---|---|---|---|
| call | 電話、電話する | button | ボタン |
| mobile phone | 携帯電話 | out | 外出中 |
| dial | ダイヤル | selfie | 自撮り、セルフィー |

**2** その他の TOEIC 頻出語句をマスターしましょう。

❶ まずは音声を聞いてリピートしましょう。 B 03

| | | | |
|---|---|---|---|
| leave | reach | operator | retrieve |
| direction | directory | extension number | request |
| return call | hold | bill | confirm |
| appointment | caller | reschedule | transfer |

❷ 上の表の中から、下線部に適切な英語を選び入れましょう。

**モノ・その他**

| | |
|---|---|
| 請求書 → ＿＿＿＿＿＿ | （電話の）発信者 → ＿＿＿＿＿＿ |
| 名簿、要覧、リスト → ＿＿＿＿＿＿ | 操作者、通信士 → ＿＿＿＿＿＿ |
| 面談の約束 → ＿＿＿＿＿＿ | 指示、道順 → ＿＿＿＿＿＿ |
| 内線番号 → ＿＿＿＿＿＿ | 折り返しの電話 → ＿＿＿＿＿＿ |

**動作**

| | |
|---|---|
| 待つ、保留する → ＿＿＿＿＿＿ | 要請する → ＿＿＿＿＿＿ |
| 転送する → ＿＿＿＿＿＿ | 予定変更する → ＿＿＿＿＿＿ |
| 確認する → ＿＿＿＿＿＿ | 残す → ＿＿＿＿＿＿ |
| （電話などで）つながる → ＿＿＿＿＿＿ | 取り戻す → ＿＿＿＿＿＿ |

# Parts 3 & 4 会話問題＆トーク問題

**攻略ポイント** **電話の聞き取り**

- 電話での会話や、留守電のメッセージなどがリスニングではよく登場します。
- 電話でよく聞く表現・語句を押さえましょう。

## 電話での会話・トークの聞き取りのポイント

- 冒頭に注意：冒頭で「**氏名・所属**などを名乗り、電話の**目的**を簡潔に述べる」ことが多い。

  This is 氏名 from 所属（会社、部署名など）.

  I'm calling to 動詞 ～.　私は～するためにお電話を差し上げています。

- 電話での決まり文句　　音声を聞いて、ディクテーションしてみよう。　B 04

  (1) Who are you (　　　　), please?　誰におかけですか？

  (2) (　　　　) on, please.　少々お待ちください。

  (3) Let me (　　　　) you to the sales department.　営業部におつなぎします。

  (4) You have (　　　　) the tech support desk.　技術サポートデスクにつながりました。

  (5) I'm afraid she is (　　　　) right now.　あいにく、ただいま外出中です。

  (6) He is on another (　　　　).　他の電話に出ています。

  (7) May I ask who's (　　　　), please?　かけているのはどなたですか？

  (8) She should be (　　　　) by 3 p.m.　午後3時までには戻る予定です。

  (9) Would you like to (　　　　) a message?　伝言を残されますか？

  (10) Could you ask her to (　　　　) my call?　折り返し電話してくれるよう彼女に頼んでくれますか？

- 3名での会話（Part 3）：電話の場面が登場。下記のようなパターンが多い。

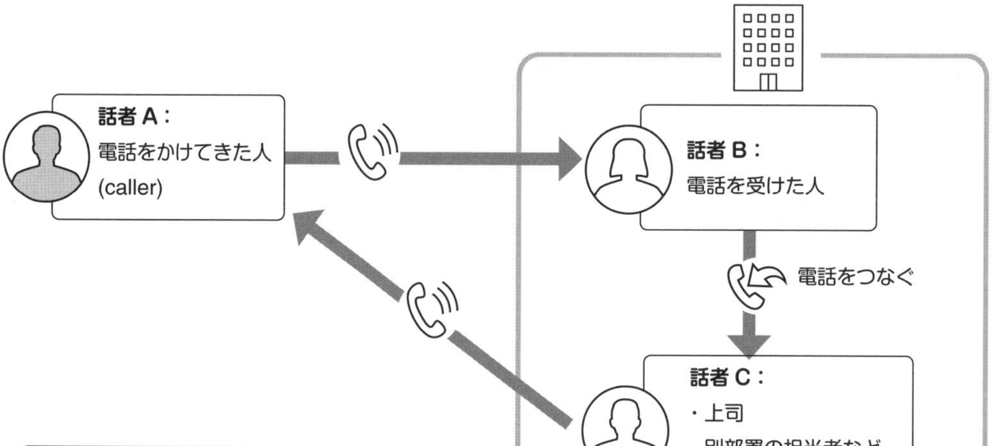


3名での会話は、Unit 14 にて練習します。

# Practice 1

Part 3 ⇒ Part 4 を 1 セットずつ連続で解いてみましょう。 B 05-06

事前に「設問」に目を通しておくことが重要(一部にのみ和訳を付けています)。

1. What does the woman say she received? 女性は何を受け取ったと言っている?
    (A) A monthly bill
    (B) An advertisement
    (C) A business number
    (D) A mobile phone

2. What does the man mention about the discount?
    (A) It is for a yearly subscription.
    (B) It is for new customers.
    (C) It is available this month only.
    (D) It is for cash payment.

3. What does the woman want to do?
    (A) Send a text
    (B) Read a book
    (C) Complete a form
    (D) See a contract

---

B 07-08

4. Where does the speaker work?
    (A) At a dental office
    (B) At a restaurant
    (C) At a hardware store
    (D) At a dry cleaners

5. What is the purpose of the call?
    (A) To give directions to the business
    (B) To request a lower price
    (C) To suggest an earlier date
    (D) To cancel an appointment

6. What is the listener asked to do? 聞き手は何をするよう頼まれている?
    (A) Clean a room
    (B) Wait for an hour
    (C) Return a call
    (D) Retrieve a message

答え合わせの前に、次のページでディクテーションをしましょう!

| No. | A B C D |
|---|---|
| 1 | Ⓐ Ⓑ Ⓒ Ⓓ |
| 2 | Ⓐ Ⓑ Ⓒ Ⓓ |
| 3 | Ⓐ Ⓑ Ⓒ Ⓓ |
| 4 | Ⓐ Ⓑ Ⓒ Ⓓ |
| 5 | Ⓐ Ⓑ Ⓒ Ⓓ |
| 6 | Ⓐ Ⓑ Ⓒ Ⓓ |

## Practice 2

各設問を解く上で重要な部分を再度聞いてディクテーションに挑戦し、和訳を完成させましょう。 B 09-14

**【No. 1】**

Hi. I just (　　　　　) my (　　　　　) for June, my third month of service.
私は6月の（　　　　　）を（　　　　　）ところなのですが、これが利用して3ヶ月目です。

**【No. 2】**

But (　　　　　) (　　　　　) receive a special discounted fee of $60
しかし（　　　　　）は60ドルという特別値引き料金をご利用いただけるのです、
for the (　　　　　) two months.
（　　　　　）2か月は。

**【No. 3】**

Can I (　　　　　) the whole (　　　　　) online?
オンライン上で、（　　　　　）全体を（　　　　　）ことはできますか？

**【No. 4】**

(　　　　　) (　　　　　) Dorothy at Logan Family **Dentistry**.
こちらはLogan Family Dentistry（=　　　　　）のDorothyです。

I'm calling about your next (　　　　　) appointment on Friday.
金曜日に入っているあなたの次回の（　　　　　）予約の件でお電話しています。

**【No. 5】**

If you'd like to (　　　　　) your (　　　　　) a day (　　　　　),
もしも1日（　　　　　）たいようでしたら、
we can certainly do that for you.
もちろんそうしていただくことができます。

**【No. 6】**

Please (　　　　　) us a (　　　　　) before Tuesday, November 3 if you'd like to reschedule.
11月3日火曜日までに（　　　　　）ください、予約変更をご希望でしたら。

前ページに戻って、答え合わせをしよう。

# Part 5 短文穴埋め問題

**攻略ポイント** 前置詞 vs 接続詞①

- 選択肢に前置詞と接続詞が並んでいたら、ここで学ぶ項目を意識して解きましょう。
- 前置詞と接続詞は、見た目では区別しにくいので、一語一語しっかり覚えましょう。

## 文法ポイント 前置詞・接続詞①

**前置詞**：名詞や動名詞（～ ing）とセットで使う [**前置詞** + 名詞（句）・動名詞]

**接続詞**：節（S+V）と節を接着する [S+V **接続詞** S+V.] [**接続詞** S+V, S+V.]

なぜ、この違いが重要？ ⇒ 同じような意味でも、使い方が異なるから。

例 私は会議に遅れました、交通渋滞**のせいで**。

前置詞 I was late for the meeting **because of** heavy traffic.（heavy traffic：名詞句）

接続詞 I was late for the meeting **because** traffic was heavy.（I：S　was：V　traffic：S　was：V）

- TOEIC に頻出する前置詞＆接続詞①：例文を参考に、どちらの品詞か考えて○を付けましょう。

| 意味＆英単語 | | 品詞 | 例文 |
|---|---|---|---|
| **原因・理由**（～だから、～が理由で） | because | 前・接 | S+V **because** it rained. |
| | because of | 前・接 | S+V **because of** rain. |
| | due to | 前・接 | S+V **due to** rain. |
| | since | 前・接 | S+V **since** it rained. |
| **譲歩**（～だけれども・～にも関わらず） | despite | 前・接 | S+V **despite** rain. |
| | although | 前・接 | S+V **although** it rained. |
| | in spite of | 前・接 | S+V **in spite of** rain. |
| | while | 前・接 | S+V **while** it rained. |
| **条件**（もし～なら） | if | 前・接 | S+V **if** it rains. |
| | in case of | 前・接 | S+V **in case of** rain |
| | in case that | 前・接 | S+V **in case that** it rains. |

**覚え方のヒント**

複数の単語がセット（＝群前置詞・群接続詞）になっている場合の品詞は、最後の単語で判断しよう。 例 in spite **of** / due **to** / in case **that**

## Practice 3

文の構造や意味を考慮して、前ページのリストから正しい前置詞・接続詞を選んで（　　）に入れ、さらに太字の部分の意味を記入しましょう。

1. The manager is not **available** today (　　　　　　　) he is taking a vacation.
   意味：

2. Guests are advised to use the emergency **stairs** (　　　　　　　) a building fire.
   意味：

3. (　　　　　　　) Ms. Patel **completed** the training, her skills were not sufficient yet.
   意味：

4. (　　　　　　　) bad weather, the annual track **competition** was canceled.
   意味：

## Practice 4

TOEIC 形式（Part 5）の問題です。空欄に入る適切な語を (A) ~ (D) から選びましょう。

解答時間：1 分 30 秒

1. ------- most of our TV advertisements are produced in China, they are broadcast mainly in South America.
   (A) Because
   (B) While
   (C) If
   (D) Despite

2. Advance arrangements will be necessary ------- you wish to pay by money transfer.
   (A) although
   (B) in case of
   (C) due to
   (D) if

3. ------- the growing popularity of online learning, many teachers are still unsure of its effectiveness.
   (A) Despite
   (B) Because of
   (C) In case that
   (D) While

# Part 7 読解問題

**攻略ポイント** **電話に関する文書**

- 電話に出た人が作成した、伝言内容のメモが文書として登場することがあります。
- 電話番号簿（社内、地域内など）をからめた問題も出題されます。
- 上述の文書によく登場する語句に慣れ、素早く読めるよう練習しましょう。

電話のメモを読んでみましょう。

## *TELEPHONE MEMO*

**To:** *Howard Tate*
**From:** *Rita Rogers*
**Taken By:** *Michael Stowe (Extension 503)*
**Time:** *Tuesday, 7 March, 2:25 P.M.*

*Ms. Rogers from Rogers Property Sales Company called. She would like to meet you tomorrow afternoon to show you the house on 3rd Avenue that she discussed with you and Bob Nelson last week. Please call or e-mail her this afternoon to set up a time to meet.*

**サンプル設問** ①まずは設問の意味を確認し、②文書からそれらの情報を探しましょう。

1. Who **answered** Ms. Rogers' call?
   (A) Michael Stowe
   (B) Howard Tate
   (C) Rita Rogers
   (D) Bob Nelson

**設問の意味**
誰が Ms. Rogers の電話 (　　　　　　)

**ヒント** 伝言の上部にある To、From、Taken by といった部分に注目しよう。

2. What **is** Mr. Tate **expected** to do next?
   (A) Confirm an order
   (B) Meet Bob Nelson
   (C) Call Extension 503
   (D) Contact Ms. Rogers

**設問の意味**
Mr. Tate は次に何をすることが(　　　　　　)?

**ヒント** Tate さんの立場（この伝言の作成者？宛先？）を検討した上で、伝言内容をしっかり読んで把握しよう。

## Practice 5

読解問題に挑戦しましょう。

**解き方の手順**

1. まずは文書の種類を確認しましょう。 directory ⇒ 名簿、リスト
2. 続いて設問を読んで「何を答えないといけないか」チェックしましょう。
3. 本文だけではなく文書の隅々にまで目を向けましょう。

Questions 3-4 refer to the following directory. 解答時間：２分

**City of Valetta**

**Phone BIZ Pages**

| Company name, Address | Telephone number |
|---|---|
| Stevens Car & Truck Repair, 101 Golden St. | 555-4710 |
| Travis Dry Cleaning, 6564 University Blvd. | 555-2944 |
| T.T.N. Fashion Boutique, 444 Grape Dr. | 555-2603 |
| Ulrich Language Institute, 54 Ellis St. | 555-1727 |
| Vernelli Italian Foods, 24B 17th Ave. | 555-2295 |

Have a local company? GET LISTED!! Make your company visible to thousands of print and online readers living nearby! To learn more and get your listing, visit www.ctyphpgs2828.com.

**3.** What is suggested about the businesses in the directory?

(A) They can be reached by train.
(B) They are located in the same city.
(C) They have online shopping sites.
(D) They have offices in the same building.

**4.** According to the directory, what can be done through the Web site?

(A) Scheduling a visit
(B) Chatting with an operator
(C) Listing a company
(D) Leaving a message

答え合わせの前に、次のページで精読をしましょう！

## 精読タイム！ 1語1語に注目しながら、正確に和訳しましょう。

### 設問の精読

3. What **is suggested** about the businesses in the directory?
   電話番号簿上の会社について何が（　　　　　　　　　　　　）？

4. According to the directory, what **can be done** through the Web site?
   この番号簿によると、何が（　　　　　　　　　　　　　　　　　）？ウェブサイトを通して。

### 文書の精読 ★重要な部分だけ！

**City** of Valetta / Phone BIZ Pages　Valetta **市** 商業施設　電話ページ

Stevens Car & Truck **Repair**, 101 Golden St. (=street)
Stevens 車&トラック（　　　　　）、Golden 通り 101 番地

Travis Dry Cleaning, 6564 University **Blvd. (=boulevard)**
Travis ドライクリーニング、University（　　　　）6564 番地

(Do you) **have a local company**? GET LISTED!!
（　　　　　　　　　　　　　　　　）？このリストに載せましょう！

**To learn** more and get your listing, visit www.ctyphpgs2828.com.
より詳細を（　　　　　　　　　　）、そしてこのリストに載せるためには、www.ctyphpgs2828.com を訪問してください。

### 選択肢の精読 ★重要な部分だけ！

3. (A) They **can be reached** by train.　それらは、電車で（　　　　　　　　　　　　　）。
   (B) They **are located** in the same city. それらは、同じ町に（　　　　　　　　　　　　）。

4. (A) **Scheduling** a visit　訪問（　　　　　　　　　　　　　　　）こと
   (B) Chatting with an **operator**（　　　　　　　　　）とチャットすること

## Reflection

Unit 9 で学んだ単語・表現をチェックしましょう。　意味がすぐに浮かぶようになるまで、反復練習しましょう。

| | | | |
|---|---|---|---|
| □ leave | □ reach | □ operator | □ retrieve |
| □ direction | □ directory | □ extension number | □ request |
| □ return call | □ hold | □ bill | □ confirm |
| □ appointment | □ caller | □ reschedule | □ transfer |
| □ dental | □ despite | □ due to | □ while |
| □ although | □ if | □ since | □ because |

# Unit 10 Construction & Landscaping

TOEIC では
- 「各種工事」「建設作業」「造園作業」などが題材として多数登場します。

この Unit では
- 「工事、作業」に関する語句・会話表現・文書などに親しみましょう。
- 文法は「前置詞・接続詞」をさらに詳しく学びましょう。

## Vocabulary Attack

**1** カタカナ語になっている TOEIC 頻出語句の音声を聞いてリピートし、意味を確認しましょう。 B 15

| | | | |
|---|---|---|---|
| glove | 手袋 | install | 設置する、パソコンにソフトを組み込む |
| tool | 道具、ツール | hose | ホース |
| water | 水、水辺<br>水やりをする | paint | ペンキ、絵具<br>ペンキを塗る、絵具で描く |

**2** その他の TOEIC 頻出語句をマスターしましょう。

❶ まずは音声を聞いてリピートしましょう。 B 16

| | | | |
|---|---|---|---|
| wheelbarrow | assemble | estimate | kneel |
| construction | appliance | invoice | stack |
| landscape | ladder | trim | brick |
| plumber | due | climb | quote |

❷ 上の表の中から、下線部に適切な英語を選び入れましょう。

**人・モノ・その他**

| | |
|---|---|
| はしご<br>→ ________ | 建築、建設<br>→ ________ |
| れんが<br>→ ________ | 予定している・期限到来の<br>→ ________ |
| 配管工<br>→ ________ | 請求書（兼送り状）<br>→ ________ |
| 電化製品<br>→ ________ | 一輪の荷車<br>→ ________ |

**動作**

| | |
|---|---|
| よじ登る、上る<br>→ ________ | ひざまずく<br>→ ________ |
| 積み重ねる<br>→ ________ | 組み立てる<br>→ ________ |
| 刈って整える<br>→ ________ | 見積もる、見積もり<br>→ ________ |
| 造園作業する、風景<br>→ ________ | → ________ |

# Part 1 写真問題

**攻略ポイント** 作業・工事現場の写真

- 写真問題によく登場する道具や装置の名称をしっかり学びましょう。
- 人物の動きや位置関係にも注意しましょう。

## Practice 1

**事前に確認** どんな単語を使って写真を表現するか、各自またはペアで思い描きましょう。
例 I see モノ in this picture. / There is (are) モノ + 場所を表す語句 .

**Step 1** 音声を聞き、写真を正しく描写している選択肢（4 択）にマークしましょう。 B 17-19

**Step 2** 再び音声を聞き、空所を埋めてから、もう一度正解を選びましょう。 B 17-19

1.

**Step 1** Ⓐ Ⓑ Ⓒ Ⓓ

**Step 2**

(A) He's (　　　　　) a (　　　).
(B) He's (　　　　　) a (　　　).
(C) He's (　　　　　) at a (　　　　　　) site.
(D) He's (　　　　　) on a (　　　　　).

2.

**Step 1** Ⓐ Ⓑ Ⓒ Ⓓ

**Step 2**

(A) A woman is (　　　　　) potted (　　　).
(B) A man is (　　　　　) bushes.
(C) A man is (　　　　　) a (　　　　　).
(D) They are (　　　　　) (　　　) in the garden.

3.

**Step 1** Ⓐ Ⓑ Ⓒ Ⓓ

**Step 2**

(A) A man is (　　　　　) on the (　　　).
(B) A woman is (　　　　　) a (　　　　　).
(C) They are (　　　　　) a (　　　　　).
(D) A woman is (　　　　　) a (　　　) to the man.

# Part 3 会話問題

**攻略ポイント** 言い換えへの対応

- Part 3 & 4 では、音声で聞こえる単語がそのまま選択肢に出てくるパターンは、全体の一部だけです。
- 多くの問題では、別の単語やフレーズに言い換えられています。
- 言い換えに瞬時に気づくことができると、正解できる問題が増えていきます。

## 言い換え表現

### 主な言い換えのパターン

**【単語⇒単語】**

音声 We'll give you ten-percent **off**. 10% 値引きします。

選択肢 (A) A **discount** 値引き

**【フレーズ⇒フレーズ】**

音声 The new software is **easy to use**. この新しいソフトは使いやすい。

選択肢 (B) It's **user-friendly**. ユーザーに優しい（＝使いやすい）。

**【文⇒文】**

音声 The hotel offers complimentary breakfast. このホテルは朝食を無料で提供します。

選択肢 (C) The guests can enjoy a free meal. 宿泊客は無料の食事を楽しめる。

breakfast ⇒ meal のように、完全な「類義語」ではないものへの言い換えには特に注意。

# Practice 2

①和訳を記入し、②言い換え語句を選び、線で結びましょう。

| 和訳 | 英語 |
|---|---|
| | call |
| | reservation |
| | grocery |
| 見積もり | quotation |
| | workshop |
| 検査する | inspect |

| 英語 | 和訳 |
|---|---|
| booking | |
| session | |
| estimate | |
| food | 食べ物 |
| contact | |
| examine | |

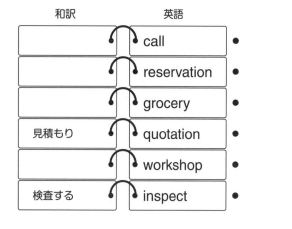

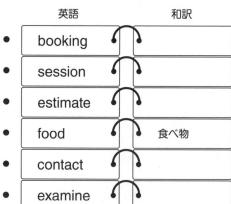

## Practice 3

Part 3 を 1 セット解いてみましょう。

事前に「設問」に目を通しておくことが重要（今回から和訳のヒントがないので、気をつけて読みましょう）。

B 20-21

1. What are the speakers discussing?
   (A) Laundry soap
   (B) A home loan
   (C) Appliance repair
   (D) Window cleaning

2. What will the man provide after the first visit?
   (A) Assembly instructions
   (B) A can of paint
   (C) Dried fruit
   (D) A price quote

3. What will they most likely discuss next?
   (A) A meeting schedule
   (B) A discount price
   (C) A new tool
   (D) A second location

| No. | A B C D |
|---|---|
| 1 | Ⓐ Ⓑ Ⓒ Ⓓ |
| 2 | Ⓐ Ⓑ Ⓒ Ⓓ |
| 3 | Ⓐ Ⓑ Ⓒ Ⓓ |

答え合わせの前に、以下でディクテーションをしましょう！

## Practice 4

各設問を解く上で重要な部分を再度聞いてディクテーションに挑戦し、和訳を完成させましょう。

B 22-24

**【No. 1】**

Our (　　　　　　) (　　　　　　) suddenly stopped working.
うちの（　　　　　　）が突然動かなくなったんです。

I heard from a friend that you provide (　　　　　　) services, too.
友達から聞いたんですけど、おたくでは（　　　　　　）サービスも提供されているんですよね。

**【No. 2】**

I can schedule a visit at your home, and then (　　　　　　) the (　　　　　　).
ご自宅訪問の予約を入れて、その後で、（　　　　　　）ことができます。

**【No. 3】**

When's the soonest (　　　　　　) and (　　　　　　) that you're available?
あなたの都合がつく最も早い（　　　　　　）と（　　　　　　）はいつになりますか？

上に戻って、答え合わせをしよう。

# Part 5　短文穴埋め問題

**攻略ポイント**　前置詞 vs 接続詞②

- 選択肢に前置詞・接続詞が並んでいたら、ここで学ぶ項目を意識して解きましょう。
- 前置詞・接続詞の区別は、見た目ではつきにくいので、しっかり覚えましょう。

## 文法ポイント　前置詞・接続詞②

### Unit 9 の復習

- 名詞や動名詞（＝動詞の～ ing 形）とセットで使う ⇒ （　　　）詞＋名詞（句）／動名詞
- 節（S+V）と節を接着する ⇒ S+V（　　　）詞　S+V.　（　　　）詞 S+V, S+V.

- 頻出前置詞＆接続詞②：例文を参考に、どちらの品詞か考えて○を付けましょう。

| 意味＆英単語 | | 品詞 | 例文 |
|---|---|---|---|
| ～の間 | during | 前・接 | S+V **during** your stay. |
| | while | 前・接 | S+V **while** you are staying. |
| ～するとき<br>～したらすぐ | when | 前・接 | S+V **when** you arrive. |
| | once | 前・接 | S+V **once** you arrive. |
| | as soon as | 前・接 | S+V **as soon as** you arrive. |
| | upon (on) | 前・接 | S+V **upon** (**on**) your arrival. |
| ～より前に | before | 前・接 | S+V **before** your arrival.<br>S+V **before** you arrive. |
| | prior to | 前・接 | S+V **prior to** your arrival. |
| ～の後で | after | 前・接 | S+V **after** your arrival.<br>S+V **after** you arrive. |
| | following | 前・接 | S+V **following** your arrival. |
| ～に関して<br>～に関する | on | 前・接 | S+V **on** your arrival. |
| | concerning | 前・接 | S+V **concerning** your arrival. |
| | regarding | 前・接 | S+V **regarding** your arrival. |

**要注意の用法**　接続詞だけれど、動名詞とセットで使うものがある(主語と be 動詞を省略する用法)。
・while **driving** (運転している間)
・when **speaking** in English　(英語で話すとき)

## Practice 5

文の構造や意味を考慮して、前ページのリストから正しい前置詞・接続詞を選んで（　）に入れ、さらに太字の部分の意味を記入しましょう。

1. The potted plants were safely **gathered** in the shelter (　　　　　) the storm came.
   意味：　　前に

2. Please do not bring any beverages with you (　　　　　) **boarding** a plane.
   ときに　　意味：

3. One of my colleagues sent me a **text** (　　　　　) a change of itinerary.
   意味：　　に関する

4. (　　　　　) we greeted each other, we walked over to the **fountain** and started chatting.
   後で　　意味：

## Practice 6

TOEIC 形式（Part 5）の問題です。空欄に入る適切な語を (A) ~ (D) から選びましょう。

解答時間：1 分 30 秒

1. The group discount applies only to those who contact us ------- their visits.
   (A) when
   (B) once
   (C) prior to
   (D) because of

2. The rules ------- street parking in the downtown area are not clear enough.
   (A) before
   (B) following
   (C) while
   (D) regarding

3. You should show your identification badge ------- entering the construction site.
   (A) concerning
   (B) upon
   (C) during
   (D) in case that

# Part 7 読解問題

**攻略ポイント** **請求書**

- 発行した業者、宛先（顧客）、請求内容（物品販売、作業、サービス）などが書いてあります。
- 送料、値引きなどの欄にも注意が必要です。
- 表の上・下にも重要な情報が書いてあることが多いので、見落とさないよう気を付けましょう。

請求書（invoice）を読みましょう。

## Dan's Home Repairs INVOICE

Client: Wendy Adams
Location: 3244 Greenway Road, Hamdon CA 90012

| Work Item | Materials cost* | Labor cost** | Subtotals |
|---|---|---|---|
| Build stone steps to back door. | $250 | $180 | $430 |
| Repair back window. | $38 | $30 | $68 |
| Install 5 garden lights. | $150 | $45 | $195 |
| Repair driveway, southwest corner. | $221 | $120 | $341 |
| Replace 2 garden hoses. | $82 | $0 | $82 |
| **Total due:** | | | **$1,116** |

*Full details available upon request.
**Labor billed at $30 per hour.

**サンプル設問** ①まずは設問の意味を確認し、②それらの情報を探しましょう。

1. Where **was** the work **done**?
   (A) At a person's home
   (B) At a public park
   (C) In a museum garden
   (D) At a resort hotel

**設問の意味**
どこで作業は（　　　　　　　　）？

**ヒント** 請求書の発行者（＝業者名）＆作業内容から読み取ろう。

2. What will **be provided** if requested by the customer?
   (A) A job application form
   (B) Information about garden lights
   (C) A list of local plumbers
   (D) Transportation to the job site

**設問の意味**
何が（　　　　　　　　）、顧客から要請があれば？

**ヒント** 表の中だけではなく外にも注意しよう。

# Practice 7

読解問題に挑戦しましょう。

**解き方の手順**

1. まずは文書の種類を確認しましょう。 invoice ⇒ 請求書
2. 続いて設問を読んで「何を答えないといけないか」チェックしましょう。
3. 本文だけではなく文書の隅々にまで目を向けましょう。

Questions 3-4 refer to the following invoice. 解答時間：2 分

**Caterina Fine Gifts of Italy**

*Verona* | *Rome* | *Paris*

| Sold to: | Ship to: |
|---|---|
| Barbara Norton<br>553 Redroy St.<br>Miami, FL 32005 U.S.A. | Thomas Cheng<br>9092 Winthrup Dr.<br>Dayton OH 43049 U.S.A. |

| **Product description, model** | **Quantity** | **Unit Price** | **Subtotal** |
|---|---|---|---|
| Gold tie pin "Spirito" | 1 | 124.50 | 124.50 |
| Silver money clip "Occasione" | 1 | 175.00 | 175.00 |
| International Shipping Invoice | | Shipping: | 28.00 |
| | | Total: | 327.50 |

(Note: All prices are in U.S. dollars unless otherwise noted.)

3. What is indicated on the invoice?
   - (A) The seller is based in the United States.
   - (B) One item needs assembling.
   - (C) Ms. Norton must pay for shipping.
   - (D) Prices are listed in Euros.

4. What is the same for both of the items purchased?
   - (A) The model name
   - (B) The function
   - (C) The unit price
   - (D) The quantity

答え合わせの前に、次のページで精読をしましょう！

## 精読タイム！

1語1語に注目しながら、正確に和訳しましょう。

### 設問の精読

3. What is indicated on the **invoice**?
（　　　　　）には何が書いてありますか？

4. What is **the same** for both of the items purchased?
何が（　　　　　）ですか？購入された品物の両方にとって。

### 文書の精読

★重要な部分だけ！

(**They were) Sold** to:　Barbara Norton
これらは～に（　　　　　　　）: Barbara Norton

| **Product description,** model | | **Quantity** |
|---|---|---|
| 製品（　　　　　）、型名 | | （　　） |
| **Shipping** | 28.00 | |
| （　　　　　　） | | |

(Note: All prices are in U.S. dollars **unless** otherwise noted.)
（注：全ての金額は米国ドル表示です、別途記載されて（　　　　　　　　））

### 選択肢の精読

★重要な部分だけ！

3. (B) One item needs **assembling**.　1つの品物は（　　　）が必要である。
   (C) Ms. Norton must **pay for shipping**.　Ms. Nortonは（　　　　　）なければならない。

4. (B) The function （　　　　　）
   (C) The unit price （　　　　　）

# Reflection

Unit 10 で学んだ単語・表現をチェックしましょう。

意味がすぐに浮かぶようになるまで、反復練習しましょう。

| | | | |
|---|---|---|---|
| □ wheelbarrow | □ assemble | □ estimate | □ kneel |
| □ construction | □ appliance | □ invoice | □ stack |
| □ landscape | □ ladder | □ trim | □ brick |
| □ plumber | □ due | □ climb | □ quote, quotation |
| □ install | □ paint | □ inspect | □ once |
| □ examine | □ regarding | □ prior to | □ quantity |

# Unit 11 Personnel

**TOEICでは**
- 「求人」や「人事（採用・異動・昇進・退職など）」が題材として多数登場します。

**このUnitでは**
- 求人や人事に関する語句・会話表現・文書などに親しみましょう。
- リーディングは「文と文をつなぐ表現」を学びましょう。

## Vocabulary Attack

**1** カタカナ語になっているTOEIC頻出語句の音声を聞いてリピートし、意味を確認しましょう。 B 25

| | | | |
|---|---|---|---|
| opening | 空き、欠員、オープニング | career | キャリア、経歴、（生涯取り組むような）仕事 |
| position | 役職 | intern | インターン |
| résumé | 履歴書 | major | （大学の）専攻 |

**2** その他のTOEIC頻出語句をマスターしましょう。

❶ まずは音声を聞いてリピートしましょう。 B 26

| | | | |
|---|---|---|---|
| seek | qualification | vacancy | candidate |
| degree | reference | apply for | benefits |
| paid vacation | submit | certificate | diploma |
| experience | temporary | hire | personnel |

❷ 上の表の中から、下線部に適切な英語を選び入れましょう。

**人・モノ・その他**

| | | |
|---|---|---|
| 候補者 → ________ | 卒業証書 → ________ | 諸手当 → ________ |
| 臨時の、一時的な → ________ | 学位 → ________ | 有給休暇 → ________ |
| 認定証、証書 → ________ | 資質、資格、能力 → ________ | 人事、スタッフ → ________ |
| 経験（する） → ________ | 空き、欠員 → ________ | 身元照会、推薦 → ________ |

**動作**

| |
|---|
| 雇う → ________ |
| 探し求める → ________ |
| 提出する → ________ |
| ～に応募する、申し込む → ________ |

# Part 2 応答問題

**攻略ポイント** **選択疑問文**

- **「Aですか、それともBですか？」という「選択疑問文」が出題されます。**
- **「正解パターン」と「誤答パターン」を学び、確実に正解しましょう。**

**選択疑問文とは**

| **WH 疑問詞を使うもの** | **WH 疑問詞を使わないもの** |
|---|---|
| How do you commute, by bus **or** by subway? | Would you like beef **or** chicken? |
| Which room did you reserve, Room A **or** Room B? | Should we advertise on TV **or** on the Web? |

**正解パターン**

**誤答パターン**⇒ Yes / No で答える。例 Yes, we should advertise on TV.

- どちらか片方だと答える　I usually use the subway. / I'd like beef, please.
- 「どちらでも」、「両方」などと答える　I reserved both rooms. / Either is fine with me.
- 「～次第である」、「まだ決まっていない」などと答える　It depends on the day. / We are still deciding.

## Practice 1

**Step 1** 「問いかけ＆その応答」を聞いて、空所を埋めましょう。　B 27-29

1. Do you plan to (　　　) summer interns (　　　) (　　　) or (　　　) (　　　)?
   — I'm (　　　) sometime early (　　　) (　　　).

2. Who's (　　　) an (　　　) (　　　), Martin or Susan?
   — (　　　) (　　　) (　　　) do.

3. Where will the (　　　) (　　　) be (　　　), in London or in Munich?
   — (　　　), I (　　　) a (　　　) in Paris.

**Step 2** 同じ「問いかけ―応答」を聞いて、適切な応答かどうか判断しましょう。　B 27-29

1. 適切・不適切　　2. 適切・不適切　　3. 適切・不適切

## Practice 2

TOEIC 形式 (Part 2) の問題を解きましょう。　B 30-32

**Step 1** 正解を選びましょう。　**Step 2** 聞き取れた単語をメモしましょう。

1. Ⓐ Ⓑ Ⓒ

2. Ⓐ Ⓑ Ⓒ

3. Ⓐ Ⓑ Ⓒ

# Part 4 トーク問題

**攻略ポイント** 人事に関するお知らせ

- 「新任」「退職」「異動」「昇進」「表彰」「新任」などを社内外に伝えるトークがよく出題されます。
- トークの中では「人名」「役職・部署名」「担当職務」「過去の経験・功績」などが語られます。
- 歓迎会や送別会の案内を含むことも多いので、気を付けて聞き取りましょう。

## 人事・役職に関する表現

- 人事に関する表現：以下の語群から選んで、空所を埋めましょう。

**transfer / celebrate / retirement / promotion / contribution**

| | | | |
|---|---|---|---|
| 任命 | appointment | 退職 | (　　　　　) |
| 異動・転勤 | (　　　　　) | 後任 | replacement |
| 昇進 | (　　　　　)<br>advancement | 功績、貢献 | achievement<br>(　　　　　) |
| 表彰する | recognize | 祝う | (　　　　　) |

- 役職名：以下の語群から選んで、空所を埋めましょう。

**full / chief / permanent / managerial / board / temporary**

| | | | |
|---|---|---|---|
| 役員 | director, officer<br>(　　　) member | 幹部、経営陣 | executive,<br>management |
| 会長 | chairperson | 最高経営責任者 | (　　　) Executive Officer |
| 本部長、副社長 | vice president | 責任者 | head, leader,<br>manager |
| 常勤職 | a (　　　)-time position | 非常勤職 | a part-time position |
| 長期雇用 | a (　　　　　) position | 臨時雇用 | a (　　　　　) position<br>a seasonal job |
| 管理職 | a (　　　　　) position | 事務職 | a clerical position |

## Practice 3

Part 4 を 1 セット解いてみましょう。 B 33-34

1. What is being celebrated?
   (A) A successful business year
   (B) An industry award
   (C) Promotion to a senior position
   (D) A colleague's retirement

2. What has Mary helped the company to receive?
   (A) A positive public image
   (B) A special discount
   (C) Necessary funds
   (D) Local government support

3. Who is Sam Gibbs?
   (A) Mary's replacement
   (B) A party organizer
   (C) The company's founder
   (D) A part-time advisor

| No. | A B C D |
|---|---|
| 1 | Ⓐ Ⓑ Ⓒ Ⓓ |
| 2 | Ⓐ Ⓑ Ⓒ Ⓓ |
| 3 | Ⓐ Ⓑ Ⓒ Ⓓ |

答え合わせの前に、次でディクテーションをしましょう！

## Practice 4

各設問を解く上で重要な部分を再度聞いてディクテーションに挑戦し、和訳を完成させましょう。 B 35-37

**【No. 1】**

We're holding this party for our senior ( ), Mary Harne,
私たちはこのパーティを、当社の上級（ ）Mary Harne のために開いています、
who is ( ) this month.
彼女は今月退職します。

**【No. 2】**

Her accurate ( ) has helped us ( ) necessary ( )
彼女の正確な（ ）が、必要な（ ）のに貢献してきました。
during good times and bad.
当社が好況不況のどちらの間も。

**【No. 3】**

Mary has helped us find and ( ) a very able ( ), Sam Gibbs.
大変有能な（ ）、Sam Gibbs を探し（ ）するのに Mary は手を貸してくれました。

上に戻って、答え合わせをしよう。

# Part 6　長文穴埋め問題

**攻略ポイント**　文と文をつなぐ語句

- Part 6 とは、文書中に設けられた空所を埋める問題です。
- 品詞、代名詞、前置詞 vs 接続詞など、問われる項目は Part 5 と変わりません。
- 文書を読むのに時間をかけ過ぎず、空所のある文を中心に読んで解きましょう。

## 解法ポイント　文と文をつなぐ言葉（副詞、前置詞＋名詞）

### 既習事項の復習（Units 9 & 10）

- 名詞や動名詞（＝動詞の～ ing 形）とセットで使う ⇒ （　　　　　）詞 + 名詞（句）・動名詞
- 節（S+V）と節を接着する ⇒ S+V（　　　　　）詞　S+V.　（　　　　　）詞 S+V, S+V.

### 文と文をつなぐ言葉（副詞、前置詞 + 名詞）とは？

直後にコンマ（,）を打てるのも特徴の 1 つ

- 文と文を接着する ⇒ S+V.　**つなぎ言葉**, S+V.

| 種類 | つなぎ言葉 | 意味 |
|---|---|---|
| 追加、補足 | in addition | （前文の内容に）**加えて** |
| | additionally | （前文の内容に）**加えて** |
| | moreover | （前文の内容に加え）**更に** |
| | similarly | （前文の内容と）**同様に** |
| | in fact | （前文の内容を受けて）**確かに , 実際は** |
| 結論、結果 | therefore | （前文の内容に）**したがって** |
| | as a result | その（前文の内容）**結果** |
| 対比、譲歩 | however | それ（前文の内容）**にもかかわらず** |
| | regardless | それ（前文の内容）**を気にせずに** |
| | nevertheless | それ（前文の内容）**にもかかわらず** |
| | instead | その（前文の内容）**代わりに、それよりも** |

同じような意味の「前置詞」「接続詞」もある。意味だけではなく、空所の前後の状況から、適切な品詞を検討しよう（次ページで練習）。

**要注意の用法**　後ろに<前置詞＋名詞／動名詞>を付ける用法もある。
- in addition **to a cash card**（キャッシュカードに加えて）
- regardless **of location**（場所にはかからわず、場所を問わず）
- as a result **of the accident**（その事故の結果）
- instead **of working on Sundays**（日曜日に働く代わりに）

## Practice 5

空所の前後の文の意味を検討して、前ページから正しいつなぎ言葉を選んで（　　　）に入れ、さらに、太字の部分の意味を記入しましょう。

1. Several buses were at the terminal. (　　　　　), only one of them was **bound for** Delhi.
   意味：

2. Free Wi-Fi is available in the lobby. (　　　　　), bring your **laptop** if you plan to work.
   意味：

3. We offer competitive salaries and benefits. (　　　　　), free **meals** are available in the company cafeteria.
   意味：

4. (　　　　　) the increased **budget**, we could advertise a job vacancy in the local paper.
   意味：

## Practice 6

TOEIC 形式（Part 6）の問題です。空欄に入る適切な語を (A) ~ (D) から選びましょう。

解答時間：1 分 30 秒

**Questions 1-2 refer to the following e-mail.**

To: Dante Weller
From: Stacy Garland
Subject: A follow-up interview
Date: July 27

Dear Mr. Weller,

Thank you for participating in our online recruiting event. Your application meets all the necessary qualifications for the current opening. ---1.---, our hiring committee has selected you for a follow-up interview to discuss the details of your current skill set. ---2.---, we would like to discuss your career goals in the context of possible employment at StatStorage Technologies. Please contact me at your earliest convenience to schedule the face-to-face interview.

Sincerely,

Stacy Garland
Personnel Department Manager, StatStorage Technologies Inc.

1. (A) Nevertheless (B) In fact (C) Although (D) Instead of
2. (A) In addition (B) Regardless of (C) However (D) Despite

# Part 7 読解問題

**攻略ポイント** 求人広告

求人広告には、簡潔に以下の内容について書いてあります。これらを意識しながら読むようにしましょう。

- 雇用主（社名、業種、所在地）
- 募集している職種・仕事内容（職務）
- 応募条件（学歴、資格、業務経験など）★必須条件＋優遇条件（必須ではないが望ましい）
- 応募方法（提出書類、提出先、期日など）

求人広告を読みましょう。

> Blaremont Analytics Co. is seeking a Market Research Team member to gather and analyze customer satisfaction information. The successful candidate must have strong personal computer and telephone communication skills. At least two years' professional customer service experience is a must. Data analysis experience or a degree in a related field would be a plus, but not required. Submit your résumé and cover letter to hiring@blaremont.com. Qualified applicants will be contacted within five days of submission.

**サンプル設問** ①まずは設問の意味を確認し、②文書からそれらの情報を探しましょう。

1. What is one of the **requirements** for the job?
   - (A) A college degree
   - (B) Data analysis experience
   - (C) Ability to lead a team
   - (D) Computer skills

**設問の意味**
その仕事（　　　　　　　　）の1つは何？

**ヒント** 応募条件には「必須」と「望ましい」がある。必須条件を探そう。

2. How should one **apply for** the position?
   - (A) By sending an e-mail
   - (B) By visiting the business in person
   - (C) By calling a Market Research Team member
   - (D) By completing an online form

**設問の意味**
どのようにその役職に（　　　　　　）すべき？

**ヒント** 応募方法はたいてい、求人広告の後半に書いてある。

# Practice 7

読解問題に挑戦しましょう。

**解き方の手順**

1. まずは文書の種類を確認しましょう。 **advertisement** ⇒ 広告
2. 続いて設問を読んで「何を答えないといけないか」チェックしましょう。
3. 本文だけではなく文書の隅々にまで目を向けましょう。

Questions 3-4 refer to the following advertisement.

解答時間：2 分

## Job Vacancies – Immediate Hiring

LoveCart Grocery Stores, a Houston-based supermarket chain, is looking for friendly, efficient people to help run the stores and serve customers well. Applicants must be ready to work in the deli and grocery sections of our stores, and to accept assignments to different store locations. A high-school diploma is required, and we will train qualified applicants who lack professional experience. We offer great benefits including a five-day paid vacation. To request an interview appointment, visit us online at www.lovecart-jobappl.com. You will need scanned images of your I.D. and diploma. References from previous employers are helpful, but not required.

**3.** According to the ad, what is required for the job?

**(A)** A food safety certificate
**(B)** Fluency in a different language
**(C)** Customer service experience
**(D)** Working at multiple locations

**4.** What should a job seeker do to make an appointment?

**(A)** Call the closest store location
**(B)** Mail a list of references to Houston
**(C)** Visit the LoveCart Web site
**(D)** Take a customer satisfaction survey

答え合わせの前に、次のページで精読をしましょう！

## 精読タイム！

1語1語に注目しながら、正確に和訳しましょう。

### 設問の精読

3. According to the ad, what **is required** for the job?
   この広告によると、その仕事には何が（　　　　　　　　　　　　）？

4. What should a **job seeker** do to make **an appointment**?
   （　　　　　　　）は何をするべきですか、（　　　　　　　）をするために？

### 文書の精読 ★重要な部分だけ！

**Applicants** must be ready ① to work in the deli and **grocery** sections of our stores,
（　　　　　　　）は～ができなくてはなりません、①総菜と（　　　　　　　）売り場で働き、
and ② to accept **assignments** to different store locations.
②別店舗での（　　　　　　　）も引き受けることが（できなくてはなりません）。

A high-school **diploma** is required
高校の（　　　　　　　）は必須です。

To request an **interview** appointment, visit us online at www.lovecart-jobappl.com.
（　　　　　　　）の予約を取るためには、www.lovecart-jobappl.com を訪問してください。

### 選択肢の精読 ★重要な部分だけ！

3. (A) A food safety **certificate** 食品安全（　　　　　　　）
   (D) Working at **multiple** locations （　　　　　　　）拠点での勤務

4. (A) Call the **closest** store location （　　　　　　　）店舗に電話する
   (B) Mail a list of **references** to Houston Houston に（　　　　　　　）リストを郵送する

## Reflection

Unit 11 で学んだ単語・表現をチェックしましょう。

意味がすぐに浮かぶようになるまで、反復練習しましょう。

| | | | |
|---|---|---|---|
| ☐ opening | ☐ position | ☐ résumé | ☐ career |
| ☐ seek | ☐ qualification | ☐ vacancy | ☐ candidate |
| ☐ degree | ☐ reference | ☐ apply for | ☐ benefits |
| ☐ paid vacation | ☐ submit | ☐ certificate | ☐ diploma |
| ☐ experience | ☐ temporary | ☐ hire | ☐ personnel |
| ☐ board member | ☐ promotion | ☐ retirement | ☐ moreover |
| ☐ therefore | ☐ however | ☐ additionally | ☐ instead |

# Unit 12 Business Ventures

**TOEIC では**
- 「新規事業」「新製品」「起業」などが題材として多数登場します。

**この Unit では**
- 「新規事業・新製品・起業」に関する語句・会話表現・文書などに親しみましょう。
- リスニングは「グラフィック問題」、リーディングは「語句の組み合わせ」について学びましょう。

## Vocabulary Attack

**1** カタカナ語になっている TOEIC 頻出語句の音声を聞いてリピートし、意味を確認しましょう。 B 38

| | | | |
|---|---|---|---|
| model | （製品の）型・様式、模型 | brand | ブランド、銘柄 |
| sample | サンプル、試す | fund | 資金、資金を提供する |
| award | 賞、賞を与える | release | 発売、発表（する） |

**2** その他の TOEIC 頻出語句をマスターしましょう。

❶ まずは音声を聞いてリピートしましょう。 B 39

| | | | |
|---|---|---|---|
| establishment | decade | merge | found |
| expand | in charge | attractive | grant |
| relocate | acquire | reward | latest |
| invite | own | entrepreneur | offer |

❷ 上の表の中から、下線部に適切な英語を選び入れましょう。

**人・モノ・その他**

| | |
|---|---|
| 起業家<br>→ ________ | 最新の<br>→ ________ |
| 助成金<br>→ ________ | 魅力的な<br>→ ________ |
| 報奨<br>→ ________ | 担当している<br>→ ________ |
| 10 年<br>→ ________ | 機関、施設<br>→ ________ |

**動作**

| | |
|---|---|
| 提供する、申し出る<br>→ ________ | 招く、勧める<br>→ ________ |
| 獲得する、買収する<br>→ ________ | 設立する、創設する<br>→ ________ |
| 所有する<br>→ ________ | 拡大する<br>→ ________ |
| 合併する<br>→ ________ | 移転する<br>→ ________ |

# Parts 3 & 4 会話問題＆トーク問題

**攻略ポイント** グラフィック問題①

- 図や表などを見ながら解く問題が「グラフィック問題」です。
- 選択肢と「グラフィック」を比較 ⇒ どの部分に目を向けるべきかが事前にわかります。
- 目線の動かし方が重要です。音声を聞くときは選択肢ではなく「グラフィック」に目を向けましょう。

## グラフィック問題

- Part 3・4 にそれぞれ 2〜3 問ずつ出題される（それぞれの Part の最後方に配置）。
- 聞き取った内容とグラフィック（図、表、グラフ、イラストなど）を照らし合わせて答える。

例 ページ下の【解き方】を確認しながら、短い音声を聞き、1 問解いてみましょう。

音声 Mr. Cheng called and said he would be late because of a traffic accident. So, we've changed the plans, and will meet him right after Ms. Kimura. B 40

**Interview Schedule**

| Applicant | Time |
|---|---|
| A. Samuels | 1:00 – 1:50 |
| C. Cheng | 2:00 – 2:50 |
| R. Kimura | 3:00 – 4:00 |
| (Follow-up calls) | 4:00 – 5:00 |

**Q:** Look at the graphic. When will Mr. Cheng be interviewed?

(A) At 1:00
(B) At 2:00
(C) At 3:00
(D) At 4:00

いつ Mr. Cheng さんはインタビューされる?

**【グラフィック問題の解き方】**

- 音声が始まる前に、グラフィックのおおまかな内容を把握します（タイトル、行・列項目など）。
- 設問 3 つのうち 1 問だけがグラフィック問題。「**Look at the graphic.**」と書いてあるのが目印です。
- グラフィック問題は、選択肢だけを見てもいても解けません。「Look at the graphic.」という指示通り、**グラフィックに目を向けながら音声を聞きましょう。**
- **選択肢に列記されているのと同じ情報**（上記の問題なら「**Time**」）**ではないほう**（上記の場合は「**Applicant**」）に目を向けるとよいでしょう。選択肢の情報をズバリ音声で述べているなら、グラフィックは不要なので、そのような問題は出ません。
- グラフィック問題以外の 2 問は、通常どおり選択肢を見ながら解きます。従って、選択肢とグラフィックの間で目線を適時に移動させることが重要です（この点を次ページで確認しましょう）。

## Practice 1

**手順を確認**

❶ 設問を３問とも読み、**グラフィック問題がどれか**確認。

❷ 図のタイトルなどを見て、**何の図であるか**チェック。

❸ グラフィック問題の選択肢と図を見比べ、**一致しない部分**を確認。

❹ グラフィック問題だけは、**目線を**「選択肢」ではなく「図（**一致しない部分**）」に置いて解きましょう。

Part 3 ⇒ Part 4 を１セットずつ解いてみましょう。

B 41-42

**City Council Meeting Schedule**

All residents are welcome to attend.

| Date | Agenda |
|---|---|
| March 26 | Beachfront cleanup initiatives |
| April 9 | Education fund |
| April 23 | Land development projects |
| May 7 | General presentations by citizens |

1. What facility are the speakers planning to relocate?
   (A) A shopping mall
   (B) An eating establishment
   (C) A warehouse
   (D) A factory

2. Where is Cully Flats located?
   (A) Near the airport
   (B) By the beach
   (C) Along a highway
   (D) Downtown

3. Look at the graphic. On what date did the man most likely attend a City Council meeting?
   (A) March 26
   (B) April 9
   (C) April 23
   (D) May 7

目線は上の図表

| No. | A B C D |
|---|---|
| 1 | Ⓐ Ⓑ Ⓒ Ⓓ |
| 2 | Ⓐ Ⓑ Ⓒ Ⓓ |
| 3 | Ⓐ Ⓑ Ⓒ Ⓓ |

B 43-44

## Nadar Electric: Research results

Table-1

| Space to cool | Rate of electricity use |
|---|---|
| One cubic meter | 400 – 600 Watts |
| One whole room | 1,500 – 2,000 Watts |
| One whole floor | 2,000 – 3,000 Watts |
| One whole home/office | 3,000 – 4,000 Watts |

**4.** Who is the speaker?

**(A)** A tour guide
**(B)** A fitness instructor
**(C)** A sales representative
**(D)** A company leader

**5.** What is a stated feature of the product?

**(A)** Low price
**(B)** Small size
**(C)** Award-winning design
**(D)** Long product life

**6.** Look at the graphic. How much energy would the GoCool You-Cooler use?

目線は上の図表

**(A)** 400 to 600 Watts
**(B)** 1,500 to 2,000 Watts
**(C)** 2,000 to 3,000 Watts
**(D)** 3,000 to 4,000 Watts

| No. | A B C D |
|---|---|
| **4** | Ⓐ Ⓑ Ⓒ Ⓓ |
| **5** | Ⓐ Ⓑ Ⓒ Ⓓ |
| **6** | Ⓐ Ⓑ Ⓒ Ⓓ |

答え合わせの前に、次のページでディクテーションをしましょう！

## Practice 2

各設問を解く上で重要な部分を再度聞いてディクテーションに挑戦し、和訳を完成させましょう。 B 45-50

**【No. 1】**

I think I've found a low-cost (                )
where we could (                ) our glass products (                ).
私、格安の（                ）を見つけたんです、
そこに当社のガラス製品（                ）を（                ）ことができると思います。

**【No. 2】**

Oh, that area is quite (                ) to the (                ), perfect for our (                )!
ああ、その地域ならかなり（                ）、私たちの（                ）にはうってつけね！

**【No. 3】**

I went to the City Council meeting last night. They (                ) to (                ) the (                ).
昨日、市議会の会合に行ったんですよ。議会は（                ）。

**【No. 4】**

As the (        ) (                ) in (                ) of product development, I'm excited to announce that ...
製品開発（                ）として、私は発表できることにわくわくしています、～。

**【No. 5】**

It's a personal, (                ) air conditioner that's as (                ) and (                ) as a briefcase.
一人用の、（                ）エアコンで、ブリーフケースくらい（                ）のです。

**【No. 6】**

Simply plug it in and it can (                ) an area of up to one (                ) (                ).
プラグを差し込むだけで（                ）できます、（                ）までの範囲を。

前ページに戻って、答え合わせをしよう。

# Part 5 短文穴埋め問題

**攻略ポイント** 語句の組み合わせ①

- TOEIC のリーディングセクションでは「語句の組み合わせ」が鍵になる問題が出題されます。
- 選択肢や問題文に、以下の語句を発見したら、ここで学ぶ項目を意識して解きましょう。
- 意味もしっかり覚えましょう。

## 組み合わせで覚えておきたい語句 ①

「意味」を参考に、選択肢の中から適切な語を選びましょう。

| | | (-----) に入る語は？ | 意味 |
|---|---|---|---|
| 1 | either A (-----) B | and / or / nor / of | A か B かどちらか |
| 2 | both A (-----) B | and / or / nor / of | A も B もどちらも |
| 3 | neither A (-----) B | and / or / nor / of | A も B もどちらも～ない |
| 4 | whether A (-----) B | and / or / nor / of | A か B のどちらであろうと<br>A か B のどちらなのか |
| 5 | between A (-----) B | and / or / nor / of | A と B の間に |
| 6 | thank 人 (-----) ～ | of / for / with / on / in / to | ～のことで人に感謝する |
| 7 | be responsible (-----) ～ | of / for / with / on / in / to | ～に対して責任がある |
| 8 | be interested (-----) ～ | of / for / with / on / in / to | ～に興味・関心がある |
| 9 | focus (-----) ～ | of / for / with / on / in / to | ～に集中する |
| 10 | sign up (-----) ～ | of / for / with / on / in / to | ～に申し込む、登録する |
| 11 | (-----) two weeks | of / for / with / on / in / to | 今から 2 週間後に |
| 12 | specialize (-----) ～ | of / for / with / on / in / to | ～に特化する、～を専門とする |
| 13 | be equipped (-----) ～ | of / for / with / on / in / to | ～を備えている |
| 14 | a wide range (-----) ～ | of / for / with / on / in / to | 幅広い～ |
| 15 | depend (-----) ～ | of / for / with / on / in / to | ～次第だ、に頼る |
| 16 | subscribe (-----) ～ | of / for / with / on / in / to | ～（定期利用）に申し込む |
| 17 | replace A (-----) B | of / for / with / on / in / to | A を B に取り換える |
| 18 | be capable (-----) ～ | of / for / with / on / in / to | ～の能力がある、できる |
| 19 | combine A (-----) B | of / for / with / on / in / to | A を B と組み合わせる |
| 20 | be eligible (-----) ～ | of / for / with / on / in / to | ～（を受けるのに）適格だ |

**覚え方のヒント** 別の品詞や似た意味の語句も、同じような「組み合わせ」になることが多い。

別の品詞 interest **in** (～への興味・関心 #8) / responsibility **for** (～への責任 #7) / thankful **for** (～に感謝している #6) / combination **with** (～との組み合わせ #19) など

似た意味 a wide variety **of** (幅広い種類の～ #14) / expertise **in** (～の専門知識 #12) / be furnished **with** (～を備えている #13) / register **for** (～に登録する #10) など

例外 thanks **to** (～のおかげで、せいで #6) / in charge **of** (～を担当していて、～について責任を持っていて #7)

## Practice 3

前ページのリストから選んで、(　　) に適切な組み合わせとなる語を入れ、さらに太字の部分の意味を記入しましょう。

1. This brand specializes (　　　　) lightweight **luggage** and travel accessories.
   意味：
2. Our two-day **workshop** covers a wide range (　　　　) management issues.
   意味：
3. Summer interns are eligible (　　　　) certain **benefits** including two paid vacation days.
   意味：
4. The **exhibition** will start (　　　　) three months, but we have not selected the venue yet.
   意味：

## Practice 4

TOEIC 形式（Part 5）の問題です。空欄に入る適切な語を (A) ~ (D) から選びましょう。

解答時間：1 分 30 秒

1. This vehicle should be ------- of carrying construction material of at least 5,000 kg.
   (A) capable
   (B) eligible
   (C) thankful
   (D) equipped

2. Ms. Milo was given full responsibility ------- raising enough funds for the merger.
   (A) of
   (B) with
   (C) at
   (D) for

3. If your friend ------ to our premium business plan, you will receive a $50 gift-card reward.
   (A) signs up
   (B) focuses
   (C) subscribes
   (D) thanks

# Part 7 読解問題

**攻略ポイント** レター

- 多くのやりとりをEメールで行う現在、レター（封書）をわざわざ送るのは、同封物がある場合や、正式な依頼・招待・推薦などに限られます。
- 差出人・受取人に「From / To」が付いていないので、間違えないよう気を付けましょう。
  Ms. / Mr. / Dear などが付いている ⇒ **受取人**、最後の署名欄の名前 ⇒ **差出人**
- レターヘッド（便箋のトップ部分）には、差出人の会社名・住所・ロゴなどが記載されていることが多くあります。

レターを読みましょう。

**Ralley Office Supply**

Ms. Laura Taylor
8788 Morena Drive
Drewisten CO 80536

Dear Ms. Taylor,

We are pleased to let you know that your recent frequent purchases qualify you for membership in the Ralley Office Supply Customers' Inner Circle. One of the member benefits is free delivery on every order of $20 or more.

This attractive rewards program is completely free. To become a member, simply fill out the enclosed postage-paid postcard, and return it to us at your convenience. We look forward to welcoming you to the Customers' Inner Circle!

Sincerely,

Ralph Ralley
CEO, Ralley Office Supply

**サンプル設問** ①まずは設問の意味を確認し、②文書からそれらの情報を探しましょう。

1. What **has** Ms. Taylor recently **done**?
   (A) Founded the Customers' Inner Circle
   (B) Expanded an office space
   (C) Paid a monthly fee
   (D) Made frequent purchases

**設問の意味**
Ms. Taylor は最近（　　　　　）?

**ヒント** Ms. Taylor が「最近」やったことを読み取ろう。

2. What **is** Ms. Taylor **encouraged** to do?
   (A) Become an entrepreneur
   (B) Fill out the postcard
   (C) Apply for a grant
   (D) Acquire a coupon

**設問の意味**
Ms. Taylor は何をするように(　　　　　　　　　)?

**ヒント** 「～してください」「お勧めです」「～したほうがいいです」といった表現に注意しよう。

## Practice 5

読解問題に挑戦しましょう。

**解き方の手順**

1. まずは文書の種類を確認しましょう。 letter ⇒ 手紙
2. 続いて設問を読んで「何を答えないといけないか」チェックしましょう。
3. 本文だけではなく文書の隅々にまで目を向けましょう。

Questions 3-4 refer to the following letter. 解答時間：2分

**Day-2Day Computer Repair**
777 Thalor Blvd.
Salmondale, WA 98012

November 10

Dr. Marina Lanner
2920 34th Ave.
Salmondale, WA 98012

Dear Dr. Lanner,

Day-2Day Computer Repair is now closer and more convenient than ever!

We are proud to announce that Day-2Day Computer Repair has opened a second location on Naito Street just north of Townsend Shopping Mall.

If your computer seems to be running slow, making strange noises, shutting down, or even if you've spilled coffee on it, we can help. Come visit us before December 1 and receive 10% off any service fee (see the map on the enclosed coupon).

Sam & Julie Day
Day-2Day Computer Repair

Enclosure

3. What is mentioned about Day-2Day Computer Repair?
   (A) It has multiple locations.
   (B) It will open on December 1.
   (C) It just released a new product.
   (D) It invited Dr. Lanner to a meeting.

4. What is included in the enclosure?
   (A) A sample product
   (B) A computer password
   (C) A product description
   (D) A map

答え合わせの前に、次のページで精読をしましょう！

## 精読タイム！

1語1語に注目しながら、正確に和訳しましょう。

### 設問の精読

3. What **is mentioned** about Day-2Day Computer Repair?
   Day-2Day Computer Repair について、何が（　　　　　　　　　　　　）？
4. What is included in the **enclosure**?
   何が（　　　　　　　　　　　　）に含まれていますか？

### 文書の精読

★重要な部分だけ！

We are proud to **announce** that Day-2Day Computer Repair has opened a **second location**.
当店は（　　　　　　）できることを光栄に感じています、Day-2Day Computer Repair が（　　　　　　）を開店したと。

**See** the map on the **enclosed** coupon.
（　　　　　　）クーポン上にある地図を（　　　　　　　　　　）。

### 選択肢の精読

★重要な部分だけ！

3. (A) It has **multiple** locations. （　　　　　　）拠点を有している。
   (C) It just **released** a new product. 新製品を（　　　　　　）したところだ。
4. (C) A product **description** 製品の（　　　　　　）

# Reflection

Unit 12 で学んだ単語・表現をチェックしましょう。

意味がすぐに浮かぶようになるまで、反復練習しましょう。

| | | | |
|---|---|---|---|
| ☐ model | ☐ award | ☐ fund | ☐ release |
| ☐ establishment | ☐ decade | ☐ merge | ☐ found |
| ☐ expand | ☐ in charge | ☐ attractive | ☐ grant |
| ☐ relocate | ☐ acquire | ☐ reward | ☐ latest |
| ☐ invite | ☐ own | ☐ entrepreneur | ☐ offer |
| ☐ specialize in | ☐ eligible for | ☐ capable of | ☐ a wide range of |

# Unit 13 Media

**TOEIC では**
- 「ラジオ」「ＴＶ番組」「報道」に関係するものが題材として多数登場します。

**この Unit では**
- 各種メディアに関する語句・会話表現・文書などに親しみましょう。
- リーディングは「パート6（文脈依存型の問題）」の解き方を学びましょう。

## Vocabulary Attack

**1** カタカナ語になっている TOEIC 頻出語句の音声を聞いてリピートし、意味を確認しましょう。 B 51

| | | | |
|---|---|---|---|
| radio | ラジオ | local | 地元の、地方の |
| commercial | コマーシャル<br>商業の、商用の | record | 記録、記録・録音する |
| studio | スタジオ | streaming | ストリーミング放送（受信しながらリアルタイムで再生） |

**2** その他の TOEIC 頻出語句をマスターしましょう。

❶ まずは音声を聞いてリピートしましょう。 B 52

| | | | |
|---|---|---|---|
| vote | annual | favorite | select |
| appear | resident | council | tune in |
| donate | introduce | concern | upcoming |
| broadcast | sponsor | survey | host |

❷ 上の表の中から、下線部に適切な英語を選び入れましょう。

**人・モノ・その他**

| | |
|---|---|
| 司会（をする）<br>→ ______________ | 年に１度<br>→ ______________ |
| 住民<br>→ ______________ | 近々起こる予定<br>→ ______________ |
| 出資・後援者<br>→ ______________ | 気がかり、心配（させる）<br>→ ______________ |
| お気に入り（の）<br>→ ______________ | 議会、評議会<br>→ ______________ |

**動作**

| | |
|---|---|
| 周波数を合わせる<br>→ ______________ | 寄付する<br>→ ______________ |
| 投票（する）<br>→ ______________ | 選択する<br>→ ______________ |
| 放送（する）<br>→ ______________ | 登場する、出現する<br>→ ______________ |
| 調査（する）<br>→ ______________ | 紹介する、導入する<br>→ ______________ |

# Part 2 応答問題

**攻略ポイント** 否定疑問文・付加疑問文

- 「否定疑問文」「付加疑問文」は一見難しそうですが、答え方はごく普通です。しっかり内容を聞き取って正解しましょう。

**通常の疑問文との違い**

例 Are you available tomorrow night? あなたは明日の夜、空いていますか？

否定疑問文 **Aren't** you available tomorrow night? あなたは明日の夜、空いて**いない**のですか？

付加疑問文 You'**re** available tomorrow night, **aren't** you? あなたは明日の夜、空いて**いますよね**？

You **aren't** available tomorrow night, **are** you? あなたは明日の夜、空いて**いないですよね**？

**応答**

通常の疑問文・否定疑問文・付加疑問文、どの形式であっても、答え方は同じでOK！

（上記の例なら）・空いている ⇒ **Yes**, I am. ・空いていない ⇒ **No**, I'm not.

したがって、疑問文の形式にはとらわれず、何を尋ねられているのかを聞くことに集中しましょう。

## Practice 1

**Step 1** 「問いかけ＆その応答」を聞いて、空所を埋めましょう。 B 53-55

1. Carol Mendez will (　　　　) at tonight's (　　　　), (　　　　) she?
   — She'll (　　　　) (　　　　) how to (　　　　) in.

2. (　　　　) the (　　　　) (　　　　) (　　　　) for the plan yet?
   — No, (　　　　) happen at the next (　　　　).

3. You (　　　　) going to the (　　　　) convention, (　　　　) you?
   — I (　　　　) (　　　　) yet.

**Step 2** 同じ「問いかけ―応答」を聞いて、適切な応答かどうか判断しましょう。 B 53-55

1. 適切・不適切　　2. 適切・不適切　　3. 適切・不適切

## Practice 2

TOEIC形式（Part 2）の問題を解きましょう。 B 56-58

**Step 1** 正解を選びましょう。　**Step 2** 聞き取れた単語をメモしましょう。

1. Ⓐ Ⓑ Ⓒ

2. Ⓐ Ⓑ Ⓒ

3. Ⓐ Ⓑ Ⓒ

# Part 4 トーク問題

**攻略ポイント** 少し複雑な設問

- Part 3 & 4 に頻出の設問をタイプ別に整理し、問われている内容をスピーディに理解できるようにしましょう。

**【話し手・聞き手が誰か?】**

| | |
|---|---|
| Who **most likely** is the woman? | 女性は（　　　　）誰・何者?（職業など） |
| **Who** is the speaker talking **to**? | 話者は**誰に**話しかけている? |

**【話の目的・主な内容は何か?】**

| | |
|---|---|
| What is the **purpose** of the talk? | この話の（　　　）は何? |
| What are the speakers mainly discussing? | 話者たちは、主に何について話している? |

**【その他、詳細情報】**

| | |
|---|---|
| **What problem** does the man mention? | 男性は（　　　　　　）のことを話している? |
| What will probably happen next? | おそらく何が起こる、次に（この後に）? |
| What is the woman **concerned** about? | 女性は何について（　　　　　　　　）? |

**【"発信者"が挿入されているタイプ】**

When **does the man say** he will appear on the show?
**男性が言うには**、彼はいつショーに（　　　　　　）予定?
（↑ Part 3 では、男女どちらの話者のセリフが鍵になるのかわかる）

What **does the speaker say** will be held tomorrow?
**話者が言うには**、何が明日（　　　　　　）予定?
（↑ Part 4 では、話者は一人なので、特に重要な情報ではない）

**【セリフの意図を尋ねるタイプ】**

**What does the woman mean when she says**, "I'd be happy to"?
"I'd be happy to" **と女性が言うとき、何を意味している**?

**Why does the speaker say**, "We have another location in downtown Osaka"?
**なぜ話者は** "We have another location in downtown Osaka" **と言っている**?

設問を読むときは"～"の中だけで OK ⇒その意味がわからなければ捨ててよし!

## Practice 3

Part 4 を1セット解いてみましょう。 B 59-60

1. What does the speaker say is the topic of today's broadcast?
   (A) Fashion (B) Online shopping (C) Fiction writing (D) Real estate

2. What does the speaker mean when he says, "Karen is an expert"?
   (A) It is expensive to hire her.
   (B) She has made the right decision.
   (C) She often appears on this show.
   (D) Her message will be informative.

3. What will most likely happen next?
   (A) A musical break will begin.
   (B) The guest will talk about her book.
   (C) The host will take calls from listeners.
   (D) A commercial will be broadcast.

| No. | A B C D |
|---|---|
| 1 | Ⓐ Ⓑ Ⓒ Ⓓ |
| 2 | Ⓐ Ⓑ Ⓒ Ⓓ |
| 3 | Ⓐ Ⓑ Ⓒ Ⓓ |

答え合わせの前に、次でディクテーションをしましょう！

## Practice 4

各設問を解く上で重要な部分を再度聞いてディクテーションに挑戦し、和訳を完成させましょう。 B 61-63

**【No. 1】**

Tonight we're going to ( ) about something we all have to ( ) with
今夜、私たちが（ ）のは、私たちみんなが（ ）しなければいけないことについてです、
sooner or later. It's ( ) ( ).
遅かれ早かれ。それは（ ）です。

**【No. 2】**

Our ( ) ( ) tonight is Karen Fecklen.
今夜の（ ）は、Karen Fecklen さんです。
She can tell you why it ( ) to you.
彼女は語ってくれます、このテーマがどうしてあなたにとって（ ）なのか。

**【No. 3】**

Karen. It's good to ( ) ( ) here.
Karen さん、この番組に（ ）うれしいです。
( ) ( ) ( ) write this book?
この本を書いた（ ）？

上に戻って、答え合わせをましょう。

# Part 6 長文穴埋め問題

**攻略ポイント** 文脈依存型の問題

- Part 6 は、Part 5 と異なり、いくつもの文から成る「文書」を読みますが、その全体的な内容（文脈）から考えないと、正解が選べない問題が一定数出題されます。
- そのような問題を「文脈依存型」と呼びます。長文読解の要素が加わり、難度が高い問題も多いのですが、解き方を知っておけば対応可能な問題もあります。

## 文脈依存型問題の解法ポイント

以下の例で確認しましょう。

**1回目** 1文だけ（つまり、**文脈がわからない状態**）で、まずは検討してみましょう**（複数正解あり）**。

語彙

1. Mr. DeClark is on ------- until next Monday.

   (A) vacation　(B) a business trip　(C) his way　(D) sick leave

代名詞

2. ------- even gave me a coupon for my next purchase.

   (A) You　(B) They　(C) She　(D) It

動詞の形

3. The online advertisement ------- new subscribers.

   (A) has attracted　(B) will attract　(C) attracts　(D) is attracted

**2回目** **文脈がわかるように**、前後に文を足しました。これで再度検討し、**正解を1つ**選びましょう。

語彙

1. Mr. DeClark is on ------- until next Monday. He's visiting a new client in Paris.

   (A) vacation　(B) a business trip　(C) his way　(D) sick leave

代名詞

2. The cashier was very kind. ------ even gave me a coupon for my next purchase.

   (A) You　(B) They　(C) She　(D) It

動詞の形

3. The online advertisement ------- new subscribers. It cost $1,000, but it was worth it.

   (A) has attracted　(B) will attract　(C) attracts　(D) is attracted

## Practice 5

TOEIC 形式（Part 6）の問題です。空欄に入る適切な語を (A) ~ (D) から選びましょう。

**Questions 1-3 refer to the following article.**

解答時間：1 分 30 秒

RIVERSIDE (April 30) The Pop Korn Cable TV Network is known for its light content including mindless comedy and 20-minute romances. But this coming season, the network is changing its image with several high-quality dramas. It is -------- (1.) first serious attempt to increase an older audience.

The first of these, "Lemuel's Crossing", is a -------- (2.) drama series now ready for streaming. Taking place during an American wild-west buffalo hunt in 1875, the story is a dramatization of the superb historical novel by Andre Steen.

According to a Pop Korn Cable TV representative, an enormous production budget, talented actors, and direction by Luke Thomas all combine to make "Lemuel's Crossing" a work of cinematic art. It -------- (3.) available for viewing in many parts of Southeast Asia in June.

1. (A) his
   (B) their
   (C) my
   (D) our

It is (?) first serious attempt ～.
「それは（?）最初の本格的な試みである」

➡ **代名詞の問題の取り組み方**
① 誰・何のことを指しているか検討する。
⇒ 空所と同じ文の中、もしくは前の文から探そう！
②性別や単数・複数が鍵になることもある。

2. (A) futuristic
   (B) tropical
   (C) historical
   (D) kid-friendly

"Lemuel's Crossing" is a (?) drama series ～.
「Lemuel's Crossing は（?）ドラマシリーズである」

➡ **語彙の問題の取り組み方**
① まずは、空所と同じ文の中で検討してみる。
② 候補が複数あるなら、前の文や後ろの文にヒントを探そう！

3. (A) is
   (B) will be
   (C) became
   (D) have become

It (?) available for viewing ～ in June.
「それは、6月に視聴可能（?）」

➡ **時制の問題の取り組み方**
① まずは、空所と同じ文の中で検討してみる。
② 候補が複数あるなら、前の文や後ろの文にヒントを探そう！

# Part 7 読解問題

**攻略ポイント** メディア関連の文書

- 記事（article）:TOEIC に出題される記事の多くは、特定の企業・業界・地域情報に関するものです。
- 報道発表（press release）：企業からマスコミに送付する「情報提供」であり、これをもとに記者が独自に記事を書く場合と、このままの内容が記事になる場合があります。
- 架空の地名や社名といった固有名詞に惑わされず、必要な情報を読み取りましょう。

報道発表を読みましょう。

**FOR IMMEDIATE RELEASE**

February 14
Contact: Clara Ives, PR Dept. 415-555-1213

Trond Universal Co., a leading manufacturer of machine belts and other mechanical products, today announced that it plans to build a second factory at Broadview Industrial Park.

Construction of the new factory building is scheduled to begin on April 24. Trond Universal Spokesperson Clara Ives said the company is doubling production capacity to handle increasing orders. "The new factory will bring at least 20 new high-paying full-time jobs to the local community," she added.

**サンプル設問** ①まずは設問の意味を確認し、②文書からそれらの情報を探しましょう。

1. **What** is the main **purpose** of the press release?
   (A) To announce a new construction plan
   (B) To promote the automotive industry
   (C) To advertise an upcoming trade show
   (D) To introduce a new official sponsor

**設問の意味**
報道発表の主な（　　　　　　　　）？

**ヒント** 最初の段落に簡潔にまとめてあるはず！その内容と選択肢を照らし合わせよう。

2. According to Clara Ives, who would **benefit from** the plan?
   (A) Park rangers
   (B) Current employees
   (C) Local job seekers
   (D) City council members

**設問の意味**
Clara Ives によると誰がこの計画で（　　　　　　　　）？

**ヒント** Clara Ives が語っている部分を探し、この計画で影響を受ける人が誰なのか探ろう。

## Practice 6

読解問題に挑戦しましょう。

**解き方の手順**

1. まずは文書の種類を確認しましょう。 **Web page** ⇒ ウェブサイト上の1ページ
2. 続いて設問を読んで「何を答えないといけないか」チェックしましょう。
3. 本文だけではなく文書の隅々にまで目を向けましょう。

Questions 3-4 refer to the following Web page. 解答時間：2分

http://tswnfm.org/programs

### TSWN FM Radio — Schedule of Programs

Here are some of the locally produced programs aired on TSWN Radio.

| Time Slot | Program Title | Description |
|---|---|---|
| Mon. – Fri. 4:30–7:00 p.m. | Jazz on the Way Home | Join DJ Angela for cool, soothing jazz sounds as you drive home from work. |
| Sat. 7:00–9:00 p.m. | OUR Music | Ed Withers plays new music from our great local music scene. Hear all-local artists before they become famous. |
| Sun. 8:00–9:30 a.m. | Live-Time Classical | Live broadcasts and recordings of the best in classical concert performances. |
| Wed. 10:30–11:00 p.m. | Mr. Laughs-a-Lot | Comedy talk and interviews by Gil Bloom, A.K.A. Mr. Laughs-a-Lot |

TSWN Radio relies on support from listeners like you. Please consider becoming a donor today.

▶ DONATE NOW!

3. What program is intended for people to listen to in their cars?
   (A) Jazz on the Way Home
   (B) OUR Music
   (C) Live-Time Classical
   (D) Mr. Laughs-a-Lot

4. What is suggested about TSWN FM Radio?
   (A) It only airs music performed by local residents.
   (B) It is sponsored and operated by the city.
   (C) Some of its programs have won awards.
   (D) It is financially supported by its listeners.

答え合わせの前に、次のページで精読をしましょう！

## 精読タイム！

1語1語に注目しながら、正確に和訳しましょう。

### 設問の精読

3. What program **is intended for** people to listen to in their cars?
どの番組が、車の中で聞く人（　　　　　　　　）？

4. What **is suggested** about TSWN FM Radio?
TSWN FM ラジオについて何が（　　　　　　　　）？

### 文書の精読

★重要な部分だけ！

**Join** DJ Angela for cool, soothing jazz sounds
DJ の Angela（　　　　　　　　）、クールで心地よいジャズの音楽を、
as you **drive home** from work.　職場から（　　　　　　　　）するときに。

TSWN Radio **relies on** support from listeners **like** you.
TSWN ラジオは（　　　　　　　　）、あなた（　　　　　）リスナーからのご支援を。
Please consider **becoming a donor** today.　（　　　　　　　　）を検討してください、今日こそ。

### 選択肢の精読

★重要な部分だけ！

4. (A) It only **airs** music performed by local residents.
この局は（　　　　　　　　）、地元住民によって演奏される音楽だけを。

(B) It **is sponsored** and operated by the city.
この局は、市によって（　　　　　　　　）され、運営されている。

(C) Some of its programs have won **awards**
この局の番組の一部は、（　　　　　　　　）を獲得した。

(D) It is **financially** supported by its listeners.
この局は、リスナーにより（　　　　　　　　）支えられている。

## Reflection

Unit 13 で学んだ単語・表現をチェックしましょう。

意味がすぐに浮かぶようになるまで、反復練習しましょう。

| | | | |
|---|---|---|---|
| ☐ vote | ☐ annual | ☐ favorite | ☐ select |
| ☐ appear | ☐ resident | ☐ council | ☐ tune in |
| ☐ donate | ☐ introduce | ☐ concern | ☐ upcoming |
| ☐ broadcast | ☐ sponsor | ☐ survey | ☐ host |
| ☐ most likely | ☐ purpose | ☐ viewing | ☐ press release |
| ☐ benefit from | ☐ intended for | ☐ financially | ☐ rely on |

# Unit 14 Entertainment

**TOEIC では**
・「娯楽（映画、音楽、演劇、イベント）」に関係するものが題材として多数登場します。

**この Unit では**
・各種娯楽に関する語句・会話表現・文書等に親しみましょう。
・リスニングは「3名トーク問題」、リーディングは「語句の組み合わせ」に注目した解き方を学びましょう。

## Vocabulary Attack

**1** カタカナ語になっている TOEIC 頻出語句の音声を聞いてリピートし、意味を確認しましょう。　B 64

| | | | |
|---|---|---|---|
| seat | 席、座らせる | audition | オーディション |
| theater | 劇場、映画館、演劇 | orchestra | オーケストラ、管弦楽団 |
| athletic | 運動（競技）の | stadium | スタジアム |

**2** その他の TOEIC 頻出語句をマスターしましょう。

❶ まずは音声を聞いてリピートしましょう。　B 65

| | | | |
|---|---|---|---|
| box office | actor | direct | vendor |
| venue | enter | celebration | auditorium |
| showing | part | booth | drawing |
| film | raffle | competition | perform |

❷ 上の表の中から、下線部に適切な英語を選び入れましょう。

**人・モノ・その他**

| | | |
|---|---|---|
| 俳優、役者 → ________ | コンテスト、競技会 → ________ | お祝い、祝賀会 → ________ |
| 販売業者 → ________ | 講堂、公会堂 → ________ | （劇場の）切符売場 → ________ |
| 会場、開催地 → ________ | 役、役割 → ________ | くじ引き、抽選 → ________ |
| ブース → ________ | 上映、上演 → ________ | → ________ |

**動作**

～に参加申込する → ________

演じる、演奏する → ________

演出する、監督する → ________

撮影する、映画 → ________

# Part 2　応答問題

**攻略ポイント　平叙文**

- 疑問文や命令文などではない文を「平叙文」といい、事実・情報・意見などを伝える文です。
- 「平叙文」の出題パターンを知り、適切に正解が選べるよう練習しましょう。

**疑問文との違い**

相手に「答え」を求めているわけではないが、「リアクション」は期待している。

| 平叙文の主な内容 | ⇒ | 相手に期待しているリアクション |
|---|---|---|
| ◆ 問題や課題の指摘<br>We are out of copy paper again. | | ◆ 解決策の提示・提案など<br>Check the storage cabinet. |
| ◆ 要望・提案・申し出<br>I'd like to rent a bike for a day. | | ◆ 応じるかどうかを回答<br>Sorry, they are all rented out. |
| ◆ その他の情報<br>The movie starts in ten minutes. | | ◆ 自分の持つ情報・感想・意見を述べる<br>We should find our seats quickly. |

## Practice 1

**Step 1**「発話 & それに対する応答」を聞いて、空所を埋めましょう。　B 66-68

1. Oh my, I forgot to (　　　　) my (　　　　) (　　　　).
   — We still have (　　　　) to (　　　　) (　　　　).
2. We should have (　　　　) (　　　　) near the (　　　　).
   — (　　　　) fifty school (　　　　).
3. This year, the orchestra will (　　　　) (　　　　).
   — I hope the (　　　　) will be (　　　　).

**Step 2** 同じ「発話ー応答」を聞いて、適切な応答かどうか判断しましょう。　B 66-68

1. 適切・不適切　　2. 適切・不適切　　3. 適切・不適切

## Practice 2

TOEIC 形式（Part 2）の問題を解きましょう。　B 69-71

**Step 1** 正解を選びましょう。　**Step 2** 聞き取れた単語をメモしましょう。

1. Ⓐ Ⓑ Ⓒ
2. Ⓐ Ⓑ Ⓒ
3. Ⓐ Ⓑ Ⓒ

# Part 3 会話問題

**攻略ポイント** 3名での会話

- Part 3の会話31セットのほとんどは2名での会話ですが、**3名での会話**も数セット出題されます。
- 基本的には2名での会話と同様に解けばOKです。

## 3名での会話のポイント

### どんな3名？

- 同僚3名（Aさん、Bさん、Cさん）
  - ▶3名での打ち合わせ
  - ▶Aさん & Bさんが話しているところに、Cさんが加わる。
- 同僚2名 ＋ 社外1名（顧客、業者、友人など）
  - ▶Aさん & Bさんが、社外のCさんを訪問して打ち合わせ
  - ▶Aさんからの問い合わせを受けたBさんが、別の部署のCさんにつなぐ（Unit 9でも紹介）

※ごくまれに、3名が全くの他人（所属がバラバラ）ということもある。

### 設問で気を付けるべきことは？

- 2名での会話の設問中では、
  - ▶「the man」「the woman」⇨ 2名のうち、どちらの話者のセリフが鍵になるかを示す。
  - ▶話者の人名（例：Jason, Ms. Kimなど）⇨ 設問中で使うことはほぼない。

例1 What does **the woman (the man)** request?
**女性（男性）**は、何を求めている？

- 3名での会話の設問中では、**男性2：女性1**もしくは**男性1：女性2**になるので、
  - ▶「the **men**」または「the **women**」も登場する。
  - ▶話者3名のうちの1人の名前（例 Jason、Ms. Kimなど）も使われることが多い。

例2 What are **the women (the men)** supposed to see next?
**女性たち（男性たち）**は、次に何を見ることになっている？

例3 What problem is **Brian** concerned about?
**Brian**はどの問題について気に掛けている？
（3名のうちの1名の名前。但し、話者たちが言及している別の人物の名前の可能性もある）

**つまり、設問から「3名トーク」が推測可能！**
設問中のthe men / women / 人名
⇨ 3名での会話の可能性が高いという目印

## Practice 3

Part 3 を 1 セット解きましょう。 B 72-73

1. What are the speakers mainly discussing?
   - (A) A plan for tonight
   - (B) A birthday celebration
   - (C) An upcoming film festival
   - (D) An old auditorium

2. Why does Julian have to work late?
   - (A) To staff a box office
   - (B) To write a review
   - (C) To conduct an office tour
   - (D) To attend a meeting

3. According to the woman, what did Tom recently do?
   - (A) Go to a theater
   - (B) Purchase a TV
   - (C) Move into a larger apartment
   - (D) Repaint his wall

答え合わせの前に、次でディクテーションをしましょう！

| No. | A B C D |
| --- | --- |
| 1 | Ⓐ Ⓑ Ⓒ Ⓓ |
| 2 | Ⓐ Ⓑ Ⓒ Ⓓ |
| 3 | Ⓐ Ⓑ Ⓒ Ⓓ |

## Practice 4

各設問を解く上で重要な部分を再度聞いてディクテーションに挑戦し、和訳を完成させましょう。 B 74-76

**【No. 1】**

Debbie and I and some other people from the (                    )
Debbie と僕と他にもあと数人、同じ（          ）の連中が
are getting (                    ) after work (                    ).
（          ）んだよ、終業後に、（          ）。

**【No. 2】**

I'll be (          ) with an online (                    ) until 8:30 tonight.
僕はオンライン（          ）で（                    ）、今夜 8 時 30 分までは。

**【No. 3】**

We're going to (                    ) old classic (                    ).
私たちは昔の名作（                    ）ことにしているの。

Tom (          ) (                    ) a huge TV.
Tom は大型テレビを（                              ）。

上に戻って、答え合わせをしよう。

# Part 5 短文穴埋め問題

**攻略ポイント** 語句の組み合わせ②

- 選択肢や問題文に、以下の語句を発見したら、ここで学ぶ項目を意識して解きましょう。
- 意味もしっかり覚えましょう。

## 組み合わせで覚えておきたい語句 ②

日本語の意味に合うように、適切な組み合わせになる語句を選んで○を付けましょう。

### 比較

| | |
|---|---|
| 1. ( slow / slower / slowest ) than ~ | ~より遅い |
| 2. the ( slow / slower / slowest ) among us | 私たちの中で最も遅い |
| 3. more ( difficult / difficultly / differ ) than ~ | ~より難しい |
| 4. ( much / more / most ) faster | はるかに速い |
| 5. as ( deep / deeper / deeply ) as ~ | ~と同じくらい… |

### 品詞・動詞の形

| | |
|---|---|
| 6. allow me ( go / going / to go ) there | 私が**行くの**を許可する（可能にする） |
| 7. I look forward to ( go / going / gone ) there. | **行くの**を楽しみにする |
| 8. I'm ( will / willing / willed ) to help | **進んで**お手伝いします |
| 9. I'm ( pleasing / pleased ) to announce | **喜んで**発表します |
| 10. ( precise / precisely) at two o'clock | ２時**ちょうどに** |
| 11. ( near / nearly ) five hundred seats | **ほぼ** 500 席 |

### 前置詞・接続詞

| | |
|---|---|
| 12. ( in / on / at ) writing | **書面**で |
| 13. We're aware ( of / for / with ) the fact | その事実**に気づいている** |
| 14. not ( unless / until / under ) Monday | 月曜日**になってから、**月曜日**以降に** |

### その他

| | |
|---|---|
| 15. ( they / them / those ) who are interested | 興味のある**人たち** |
| 16. ( meet / see / watch ) expectation | 期待**に応える、満たす** |
| 17. a ( sharp / deep / keep ) increase | **急激な**増加 |
| 18. ( rise / raise / race ) funds | 資金を**調達する** |

## Practice 5

組み合わせになる語を意識して、(　　)に適切な語を入れ、さらに太字の部分の意味を記入しましょう。

1. Members are allowed (　　　　　) **the bulletin board** in the fitness center lobby.
   使う　　意味：

2. (　　　　　) who have registered early can receive a shopping **voucher**.
   人たち　　意味：

3. The number of **career** fair attendees was not as (　　　　　) as we expected.
   意味：　　大きい

4. According to the **attendant**, the film showing will start (　　　　　) at noon.
   意味：　　ちょうど、正確に

## Practice6

TOEIC 形式（Part 5）の問題です。空欄に入る適切な語を (A) ~ (D) から選びましょう。

解答時間：1 分 30 秒

1. *Behind the Curtain* was the ------- movie at the global box office in the last decade.
   (A) successful
   (B) more successful
   (C) most successful
   (D) successfully

2. The History Museum will host a special event to ------- money for a local scholarship fund.
   (A) meet
   (B) raise
   (C) perform
   (D) enter

3. The Melrose Theater Company ------- to inform you that we have selected you as the main character in our next drama.
   (A) please
   (B) pleased
   (C) is pleasing
   (D) is pleased

# Part 7　読解問題

**攻略ポイント**　NOT 問題

- 問題文の中に大文字の **NOT** があれば要注意です。「～で**ない**ものはどれか」という問いなので、文書に書いてある内容とは**異なる選択肢（もしくは書いていない選択肢）**を選びます。
- 4 つの選択肢全てを検討しなくては解けない場合が多く、時間が余計にかかる問題です。
- NOT 問題は後回しにしても OK です。そして、わからなければ無理しないことが重要です。

告知文（notice）を読みましょう。

> **Attention Local Animal Lovers!!**
> **Be a part of the**
> **Rose Heights Neighborhood Pet Show!**
>
> Scheduled for July 28 – Aug 1, this year's fair will be held at Westerly Dog Park. For only $10 a person (aged over 14), you can enjoy:
>
> - Dog & Cat Beauty Contests
> - Free training workshops (open to all dog breeds)
> - Giveaways & Raffles
> - Unusual Pet Meet & Greet (from wombats to tarantulas! Come say "Hello"), ... and more!
>
> For details on all the events, visit www.rosheightspetlove.com. You can also register your pet online to participate in an event.

**サンプル設問**　①まずは設問の意味を確認し、②文書からそれらの情報を探しましょう。

1. What **is NOT indicated** about the Rose Heights Neighborhood Pet Show?
   (A) It is a one-day event.
   (B) It includes a prize drawing.
   (C) It shows how to train your dog.
   (D) Its admission is free for small children.

**設問の意味**
Rose Heights Neighborhood Pet Show について
(　　　　　　　　　　　　　　　　)？

**ヒント**　NOT 問題なので、このペットショーについて「書いていないこと、正しくないこと」を1つ選ぶ。

2. **What can be done** on the Web site?
   (A) Finding a pet clinic nearby
   (B) Chatting with an event organizer
   (C) Making an advance payment
   (D) Entering a cat in a contest

**設問の意味**
ウェブサイト上で（　　　　　　　　　　）？

**ヒント**　ウェブサイトについて書いてあるところを中心に読み、選択肢と見比べよう。

# Practice 7

読解問題に挑戦しましょう。

**解き方の手順**

1. まずは文書の種類を確認しましょう。 notice ⇒ お知らせ
2. 続いて設問を読んで「何を答えないといけないか」チェックしましょう。
3. 本文だけではなく文書の隅々にまで目を向けましょう。

Questions 3-4 refer to the following notice.

解答時間：2分

**Mt. Rosario High School Parents**
**The Mt. Rosario High School Drama Club Needs YOU**

The annual Drama Club performance of *All About Ronnie* is only two months away, and we need your help. Volunteers will be asked to:

- ♦ Change stage settings between scenes
- ♦ Help the players put on costumes and stage makeup
- ♦ Operate theater and stage lighting
- ♦ Serve as ushers, helping guests find their seats
- ♦ Distribute show programs to guests

We can't do it without you, so please e-mail Drama Club President Meg Wilson at megwils4343@hold4mail.com to get involved.

3. What is the purpose of the notice?
   (A) To ask for help in staging a drama
   (B) To request donations for a theater event
   (C) To invite parents to watch a play
   (D) To encourage students to join a club

4. What is NOT mentioned as one of the duties for volunteers?
   (A) Lighting the theater
   (B) Helping actors into their costumes
   (C) Directing the stage performance
   (D) Providing guests with programs

答え合わせの前に、次のページで精読をしましょう！

## 精読タイム！

1語1語に注目しながら、正確に和訳しましょう。

### 設問の精読

3. **What is the purpose** of the notice?
   この通知の（　　　　　　　　　　　）？

4. **What is NOT mentioned** as one of the **duties** for volunteers?
   ボランティアの（　　　　　）の1つとして（　　　　　　　　　　　　　　　）？

### 文書の精読 ★重要な部分だけ！

We need your help. Volunteers will **be asked** to:
私たちには皆さんの手助けが必要です。ボランティアは～するよう（　　　　　　　　　　）：

- ♦ Change stage settings **between scenes**　（　　　　　　）、舞台装置を変える
- ♦ Help the **players** put on costumes and stage makeup
  （　　　　　　）が衣装着用や舞台化粧するのを手伝う
- ♦ Operate theater and stage **lighting**　劇場と舞台の（　　　　　）を操作する
- ♦ Serve as ushers, helping guests **find their seats**
  客席案内係を務め、観客が（　　　　　　　　）のを手伝う
- ♦ **Distribute** show programs to guests　ショーのプログラムを観客に（　　　　　）

### 選択肢の精読 ★重要な部分だけ！

3. (A) To **ask for** help in **staging** a drama
   芝居を（　　　　　）手伝いを（　　　　　　）こと

   (B) To **request donations** for a theater event
   劇場の行事のために（　　　　　　　　　）こと

4. (C) **Directing** the stage performance　舞台公演を（　　　　　　）こと

   (D) **Providing** guests with programs　観客にプログラムを（　　　　　　）こと

# Reflection

Unit 14 で学んだ単語・表現をチェックしましょう。　意味がすぐに浮かぶようになるまで、反復練習しましょう。

| | | | |
|---|---|---|---|
| ☐ theater | ☐ athletic | ☐ direct | ☐ vendor |
| ☐ box office | ☐ actor | ☐ celebration | ☐ auditorium |
| ☐ venue | ☐ enter | ☐ booth | ☐ drawing |
| ☐ showing | ☐ part | ☐ competition | ☐ perform |
| ☐ film | ☐ raffle | ☐ pleased to do | ☐ precisely |
| ☐ those who | ☐ raise funds | ☐ in writing | ☐ duty |

# Unit 15 Publishing

TOEIC では
- 「出版物」「出版・編集」に関係する業務などが題材として多数登場します。

この Unit では
- 「出版物や出版・編集関係」に関する語句・文書などに親しみましょう。
- リスニングは「グラフィック問題」、リーディングは「文挿入問題の解き方」と「ダブル・トリプルパッセージの解き方」を学びましょう。

## Vocabulary Attack

**1** カタカナ語になっている TOEIC 頻出語句の音声を聞いてリピートし、意味を確認しましょう。 B 77

| | | | |
|---|---|---|---|
| photo | 写真 | fair | フェア、見本市，博覧会 |
| guide | 案内本、案内係 | printer | 印刷機、印刷業者 |
| writer | 作家 | novel | 小説 |

**2** その他の TOEIC 頻出語句をマスターしましょう。

❶ まずは音声を聞いてリピートしましょう。 B 78

| | | | |
|---|---|---|---|
| issue | article | signing | autograph |
| critic | author | proofread | postpone |
| deadline | journal | copyright | publisher |
| chapter | editor | draft | explain |

❷ 上の表の中から、下線部に適切な英語を選び入れましょう。

**人・業者**

著者、(本を) 著す
→ ＿＿＿＿＿＿

編集者
→ ＿＿＿＿＿＿

批評家、評論家
→ ＿＿＿＿＿＿

出版社
→ ＿＿＿＿＿＿

**モノ・その他**

締切、期日
→ ＿＿＿＿＿＿

原稿、下書き (を書く)
→ ＿＿＿＿＿＿

章
→ ＿＿＿＿＿＿

著作権
→ ＿＿＿＿＿＿

記事、論文
→ ＿＿＿＿＿＿

[有名人の] サイン (を書く)
→ ＿＿＿＿＿＿

専門誌
→ ＿＿＿＿＿＿

署名・調印すること
→ ＿＿＿＿＿＿

**動作**

説明する
→ ＿＿＿＿＿＿

校正する
→ ＿＿＿＿＿＿

延期する
→ ＿＿＿＿＿＿

発行する、(発行物の) 号・版
→ ＿＿＿＿＿＿

# Parts 3 & 4 会話問題＆トーク問題

**攻略ポイント** グラフィック問題②

- グラフィックとそれに係る問題や選択肢には事前に目を向けておくのが大切です。
- 「位置関係」「形状」「サイズ」などを表す語句は逃さず聞き取りましょう。

## 「地図・見取り図」「イラスト」を使ったグラフィック問題

**グラフィック問題の概要・解き方 ⇒ Unit 12 で確認しましょう。**

解く手順を確認しながら、次のグラフィック問題（見取り図）を説いてみましょう。 B 79

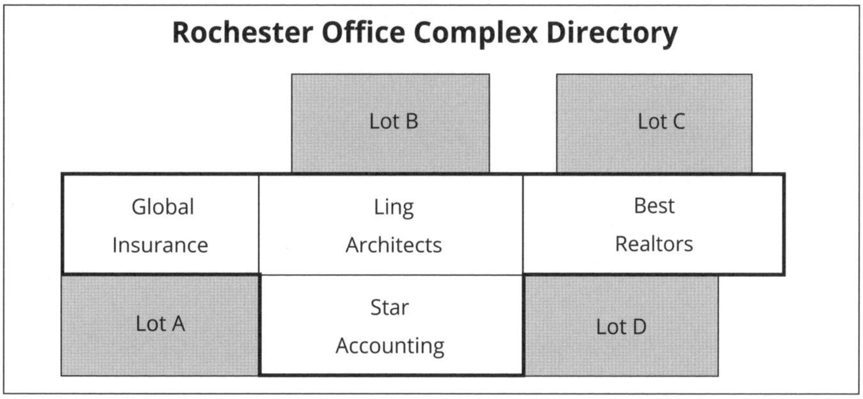


**Q:** Look at the graphic. What business does the speaker work for?

**(A)** Global Insurance　　**(C)** Best Realtors

**(B)** Ling Architects　　**(D)** Star Accounting

話者が勤めているのはどの事業所？（事前に、選択肢と見取り図を見比べよう）

英文スクリプト 難易度を上げたい人は隠して聞きましょう。 B 79

When you park your car, please use Lot B. That's the closest to our office.

**攻略法（地図、見取り図、イラストなどを含む場合）**

- 「位置関係」「形状」「サイズ」などを表す語句の聞き取りが鍵になります。
- 以下の頻出語句をしっかり覚えましょう（空所を埋めてからチェック）。

| | | | |
|---|---|---|---|
| next to ～ | ～の（　　　） | on the right (left) | 右（左）側に |
| in front of ～ | ～の前に | behind ～ | ～の（　　　） |
| on top of ～ | ～の（　　　）部に | at the bottom of ～ | ～の下部に |
| the closest to ～ | ～に最も（　　　） | the farthest from ～ | ～から最も遠い |
| round | 円形（の） | square | （　　　）形（の） |
| oval | 楕円、卵型（の） | triangle | （　　　）形（の） |

# Practice 1

Part 3 ⇒ Part 4 を 1 セットずつ解きましょう。 B 80-81

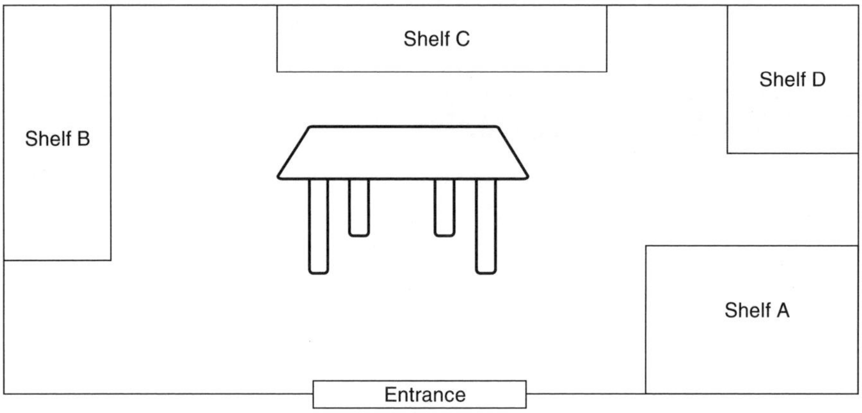


1. What event are the speakers preparing for?
   (A) A product launch
   (B) A trade exhibition
   (C) A grand opening of a store
   (D) An editorial staff meeting

2. Look at the graphic. What display does the woman want to expand?
   (A) Shelf A
   (B) Shelf B
   (C) Shelf C
   (D) Shelf D

3. According to the man, what kind of books are highly popular among their customers?
   (A) Textbooks
   (B) Travel guides
   (C) Novels
   (D) Cookbooks

| No. | A B C D |
|---|---|
| 1 | Ⓐ Ⓑ Ⓒ Ⓓ |
| 2 | Ⓐ Ⓑ Ⓒ Ⓓ |
| 3 | Ⓐ Ⓑ Ⓒ Ⓓ |

(B) 82-83

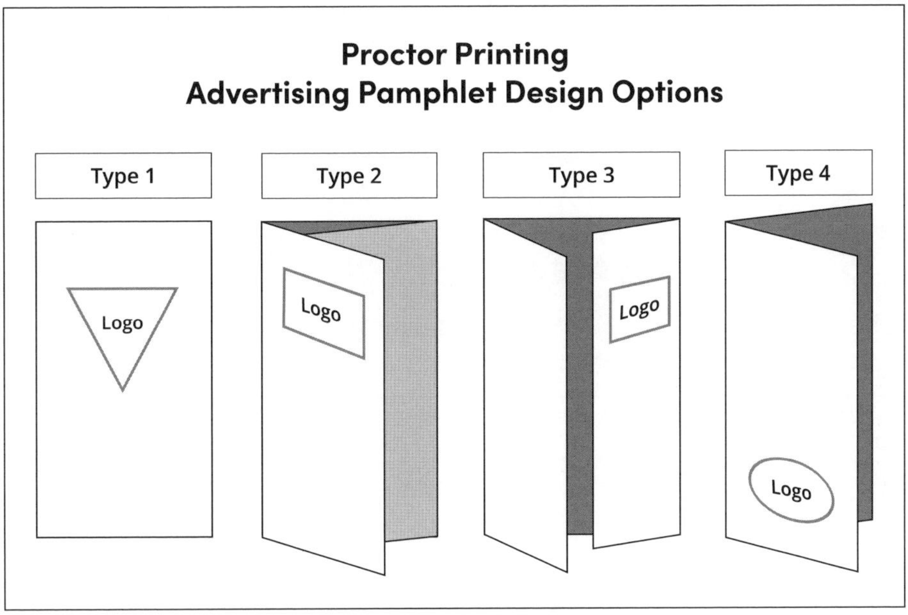


4. What does the speaker say will start next month?
   (A) Construction of a public park
   (B) A landscaping contract
   (C) A promotional campaign
   (D) Employee training sessions

5. Look at the graphic. Which brochure design does the speaker prefer?
   (A) Type 1
   (B) Type 2
   (C) Type 3
   (D) Type 4

6. What does the speaker ask about?
   (A) Price discounts
   (B) A job completion date
   (C) Regular business hours
   (D) A phone number

| No. | A B C D |
|---|---|
| 4 | Ⓐ Ⓑ Ⓒ Ⓓ |
| 5 | Ⓐ Ⓑ Ⓒ Ⓓ |
| 6 | Ⓐ Ⓑ Ⓒ Ⓓ |

答え合わせの前に、次のページでディクテーションをしましょう！

## Practice 2

各設問を解く上で重要な部分を再度聞いてディクテーションに挑戦し、和訳を完成させましょう。 B 84-89

**【No. 1】**

How is the (　　　　　) for our company's (　　　　　) coming?
当社の（　　　　　　　）の進み具合はどう？

The Publishers' (　　　　　) (　　　　　) is less than a month away.
「出版業界（　　　　　）」まで、１ヶ月を切っているわよ。

**【No. 2】**

And right (　　　　　) the (　　　　　) is our main display shelf.
そしてこの（　　）のすぐ（　　　）が、私たちのメインの展示棚です。

I think we should (　　　　　) the main shelf, since the holiday season is coming.
このメインの棚を（　　　）すべきだと思うわ、休暇シーズンが近づいているんだから。

**【No. 3】**

(　　　　　) that popular movies are based on　人気映画の原作（　　）は、
are always a (　　　　　) with our customers.
常に、当社のお客様の（　　　　）の１つですから。

**【No.4】**

We're going to start　当社は始める予定です、
our (　　　　　) door-to-door (　　　　　) campaign next month.
（　　　）戸別訪問（　　　　）キャンペーンを、来月。

**【No. 5】**

I prefer the one on the far (　　　　　).　私は一番（　　）のが気に入りました。

It's a half-fold sheet with the company logo in an (　　　　　)
２つ折りにした紙で、（　　　）形の中に会社のロゴが入っていて、
on the (　　　　　) of the front page.　表紙の（　　）部にあります。

**【No. 6】**

I need to know whether I can get them by the (　　　　　) of this month.
私は確認する必要があります、今月の（　　　）までに受け取れるかどうか。

And let me know if this (　　　　　) works for you.
そして知らせてください、この（　　　）があなたにとって都合がよいか（対応可能か）どうか。

前ページに戻って、答え合わせをしよう。

# Part 6　長文穴埋め問題

**攻略ポイント**　文挿入問題

- Part 6では、文と文の間に空所があり、そこに入れるべき「センテンス（文）」を選ぶ問題が出題されます。
- これを解くには、空所の**前後の文**との関わりに気を付けましょう。

## 文挿入問題のポイント

日本語の例で確認してみましょう。

(-----①-----)。販売部数の減少などで出版の継続が困難になったことが主な原因と述べています。『Beans』は、世界各国の珈琲豆や焙煎・抽出法を紹介し、バリスタの日本一を決めるコンテストも主催してきました。(-----②-----)。

最終号は全300ページと、通常の1.5倍のページ数を予定しています。(-----③-----)。但し、部数が限られているので、事前の予約が望ましいと担当者は述べています。

①に入るのは、**後の文につながる導入**です。例えば：

珈琲ラバー社は15日、月刊誌『Beans』を5月号で休刊すると発表しました。

↑この一文がなければ、**後ろの文**が何の原因について述べているのかわからない。

②に入るのは、**前の文に対する補足や追加情報**です。例えば：

この職業の認知度を高めたのは、この雑誌の功績の1つです。

↑**前の文**から「この職業＝バリスタ」のことだとわかる。

③に入るのは、**前と後ろの文をつなぐ情報**です。例えば：

価格は通常通り1100円で、大手書店やオンライン書店等で販売されます。

↑**前の文**から「最終号の価格」のことだとわかる。

↑この文があることで、**後ろの文**の「部数」「事前の予約」への流れもスムーズである。

このように、文書の内容が読み取れれば、自然に「どの文を入れるべきか」を判断できますが、単語などが難しくて文書の内容がわからないときは、かなり難しく感じます。その場合は、無理に解く必要はないので、適当な答えを選んでおきましょう。Part 6（全16問）の中で、この「文挿入」問題は4問だけ（1つの文書当たり1問×4文書を読む）です。

# Practice 3

TOEIC 形式（Part 6）の問題です。空欄に入る適切な語を (A) ~ (D) から選びましょう。

**Questions 1-4 refer to the following article:**

解答時間：2 分 30 秒

> When major publishing house Skinner & Dacks --1.-- its buy-out of Trigger Books, a small start-up publisher, many industry watchers were surprised by the decision. --2.--, the move has proven quite successful. Trigger Books has built a solid reputation for finding new talent. Gaylon Harp, Wendy Rees and Tony Tang are among the --3.-- who became famous after Trigger discovered them. Later this month, they are planning to release *the Planetarium*, a science fiction adventure novel authored by 18-year-old Skyler Kravitz. --4.--. Reviews of advance copies are mostly positive, suggesting that Trigger Books has picked another winning talent.

**1.** **(A)** announces
**(B)** announcing
**(C)** announced
**(D)** will announce

> **時制の問題の取り組み方**
> ① 空所と**同じ文**の中で検討しましょう。
> ② 候補が複数ある場合は、**前の文**や**後ろの文**にヒントを探しましょう。

**2.** **(A)** However
**(B)** Additionally
**(C)** Therefore
**(D)** Despite

> **文と文をつなぐ語句の問題の取り組み方**
> ① 空所と同じ文の中で検討し、選択肢の中に適切でない品詞があれば除外しましょう。
> ② **前の文**や**後ろの文**の意味から検討しましょう。

**3.** **(A)** writers
**(B)** editors
**(C)** actors
**(D)** directors

> **語彙の問題の取り組み方**
> ① 空所と**同じ文**の中で検討してみましょう。
> ② 候補が複数ある場合は、**前の文**や**後ろの文**にヒントを探しましょう。

**4.** **(A)** Critics have not made any comment yet.
**(B)** She will finish her first draft soon.
**(C)** The book was popular among young readers.
**(D)** This nearly 500-page book is her debut novel.

> **文挿入問題の取り組み方**
> ①まずは空所の**直前の文**からの流れを検討しましょう。
> ② 選べない場合は、**後ろの文**にヒントを探しましょう。

# Part 7 読解問題

**攻略ポイント** ダブル・トリプルパッセージ

- 1つの文書を読んで答えるタイプを「シングル」パッセージと呼ぶのに対し、2つの文書は「ダブル」、3つの文書は「トリプル」パッセージの問題と呼ばれます。
- それぞれの文書は短いので、焦らず、シングルと同じように解けばOKです。
- 1つの文書を読むだけでは情報が足らず、別の文書からも情報収集をすることで解ける問題は、ダブル・トリプル特有です。
  ⇒ **相互参照問題（クロスリファレンス問題）**と呼ばれます。
- 相互参照問題（クロスリファレンス問題）**以外**を優先して解くことがお勧めです。
  ⇒ 多くの場合、設問文中に「どちらの**文書を読めばよいか**」が明記されている問題がそれに該当します。

## ダブル・トリプルパッセージの解法ポイント

ダブルパッセージを例にとると：

Questions 176-180 refer to the following **e-mail and notice**.

To: Eva Geraldton
From: Su Ning Goh
Subject: Book reviews
Date: July 20

Regards,
Su Ning

To regular contributors:

Before you submit your reviews, please make sure of the following points:

1.
2.
3.

176. What is the purpose of the **e-mail**?

177. What is Ms. Geraldton asked to do?

178. In **the notice**, the word "submit" in Paragraph 1, line 1 is closest in meaning to:

179. What is NOT indicated as a requirement for submission?

180. Who should be responsible for proofreading?

**文書1だけで解けそうなのは？**
Q 176・177・178・179・180

**文書2だけで解けそうなのは？**
Q 176・177・178・179・180

# Practice 4

読解問題に挑戦しましょう。

**解き方の手順**

1. まずは文書の種類を確認しましょう。 **e-mail and schedule** ⇒ Eメールとスケジュール
2. 続いて設問を読んで「解きやすそうな問題（＝どちらの文書を読めばよいかが明記されている問題）」をチェックし、それらを中心に解きましょう。
3. 本文だけではなく文書の隅々にまで目を向けましょう。

Questions 1-5 refer to the following e-mail and schedule. （解答時間：5分）

To: Eric Pierson <epierson@ze-mail.com>
From: Francine Cooper <fcooper@fremontpublishing.com>
Subject: Tour Itinerary
Date: July 20, 8:23 p.m.
Attachment: Itinerary

Eric,

Attached you'll find the revised itinerary for the first half of our upcoming book tour. As you can see, we depart on August 23. I have extended our stay in your parents' hometown to August 25-26, as you requested. This gives you extra time to visit them. I am still working on confirming the details of your press interviews and bookstore signing events during the first week of September. I'll update you on that tomorrow. In any case, I'll have you back in New York by September 8 — I promise!

Regards,

Francine

### Eric Pierson's promotional tour schedule

| Dates | Location | Time | Event |
|---|---|---|---|
| Aug. 23 | New York, New York | 2:00–4:00 p.m. | Bookstore signing & press interviews |
| Aug. 24 | Atlanta, Georgia | 2:30–4:30 p.m. | Brief talk and bookstore signing event |
| Aug. 25–26 | Cincinnati, Ohio | 10:00 a.m.–noon (daily) | Book signing events |
| Aug. 27 | Austin, Texas | 3:00–5:00 p.m. | Brief talk and bookstore signing event |
| Aug. 28–29 | Los Angeles, California | 4:00–6:00 p.m. (daily) | Press interviews with reviewers |
| Aug. 30 | Seattle, Washington | 2:00–5:00 p.m. | Informal Q&A sessions with fans |
| Aug. 31 | Chicago, Illinois | 3:30–6:00 p.m. | Brief talk and bookstore signing event |

1. What does the e-mail indicate about the upcoming trip?

(A) It is intended to support small bookstores.
(B) It involves travel by railway and air.
(C) It has been postponed by one month.
(D) The September schedule is not fixed yet.

2. In the e-mail, the word "update" in paragraph 1, line 5, is closest in meaning to

(A) direct
(B) inform
(C) accept
(D) respect

3. According to the schedule, what will happen on August 30?

(A) A new chapter will be completed.
(B) The September issue will be out.
(C) Autographs will be sent out to Seattle.
(D) Mr. Pierson will answer questions from his readers.

4. In what city do Mr. Pierson's parents live?

(A) New York
(B) Cincinnati
(C) Los Angeles
(D) Seattle

5. What is true about their plan in Los Angeles?

(A) No event is scheduled in the morning.
(B) Mr. Pierson will proofread a press release draft.
(C) Ms. Cooper will explain copyright fees.
(D) A photo shoot with fans will take place.

答え合わせの前に、次のページで
精読をしましょう！

## 精読タイム！

1語1語に注目しながら、正確に和訳しましょう。

### 設問の精読

1. **What** does the e-mail **indicate** about the upcoming trip?
   Eメールは、次の旅行について（　　　　　　　　）？
2. In the e-mail, the word "update" in paragraph 1, line 5, is **closest in meaning** to
   Eメールの中の、第1段落・5行目にある update に（　　　　　　　　）のは
3. **According to** the schedule, **what will happen** on August 30?
   日程表（　　　　　　　　）、8月30日に（　　　　　　　　）予定？

### 文書の精読　★重要な部分だけ！

I am still working on **confirming** the **details** of your press interviews
私はまだ（　　　　　）を（　　　　　）中です、記者会見と
and bookstore **signing events** during the first week of September.
書店での（　　　　　　　　）の［詳細を］、9月の第1週の分の。

I'll **update** you on that tomorrow.
それについての（　　　　　　　　　　）、あなたに明日。

Informal **Q&A sessions** with fans
ファンとの非公式な（　　　　　　　　）

### 選択肢の精読　★重要な部分だけ！

1. (C) It has been **postponed** by one month.　1か月間（　　　　）された。
   (D) The September schedule is not **fixed** yet.　9月の予定はまだ（　　　　）ない。
3. (A) A new **chapter** will be completed.　新しい（　　　　）が完成する。
   (B) The September **issue** will be out.　9月（　　　　）が発行される。

# Reflection

Unit 15で学んだ単語・表現をチェックしましょう。　意味がすぐに浮かぶようになるまで、反復練習しましょう。

| | | | |
|---|---|---|---|
| □ issue | □ article | □ signing | □ autograph |
| □ critic | □ author | □ proofread | □ postpone |
| □ deadline | □ editor | □ copyright | □ publisher |
| □ chapter | □ journal | □ draft | □ explain |
| □ novel | □ fair | □ behind | □ square |
| □ on the right | □ bottom | □ closest | □ inform |

# TOEIC Listening & Reading Test 受験時のチェックリスト

## 1 週間前には

| 済☑ | やること | 留意点 |
|---|---|---|
| □ | 受験票の到着を確認 | 未着なら、TOEIC 申込サイトにログインし、「申込履歴」⇒「受験票情報詳細」でも同様の内容を確認できる。 |
| □ | 試験会場への行き方を調べる | 試験会場は、受験票の裏に記載されている。 |
| □ | 証明写真を用意する | 細かい規定あり。詳細は受験票をチェック。 |
| □ | 本人確認書類を用意する | |
| □ | 腕時計を用意する（スマホ、スマートウォッチ、置時計などは不可） | 試験会場には壁時計が設置されてないため、必ず持参しよう。 |
| □ | 直前の受験対策として<br>・今までの学んだことを復習<br>・各パートの試験内容を確認 | 本書の他には、TOEIC 公式サイトや公式問題集などで確認するのがお勧め。<br>https://www.iibc-global.org/toeic/test/lr/about.html |

## 受験日の前日 or 当日は

| 済☑ | やること | 留意点 |
|---|---|---|
| □ | 持ち物チェック<br>・受験票<br>・証明写真（受験票に貼付）<br>・本人確認書類<br>・腕時計<br>・鉛筆 or シャーペン、消しゴム<br>・マスク | ・寒さ・暑さに弱い方は、温度調整できる服やアイテムも用意しよう（重ね着、カイロなど）。<br>・受験票未着の場合も、証明写真は必須。<br>・筆記用具は２つずつ用意。 |
| □ | 試験会場への出発時間を再確認 | 遅くとも受付終了時刻の 30 分前（試験開始時刻の１時間前）くらいに到着するのがお勧め。 |

## 試験会場では

| 済☑ | やること | 留意点 |
|---|---|---|
| □ | トイレは早めに！混雑しがち（試験開始時刻の 30 分前までには済ませて教室に戻りましょう） | 但し緊急事態なら、試験官に挙手で伝えよう。リスニングの試験時間以外であれば対応してくれる。 |
| □ | 試験前には軽く糖分補給（脳に栄養） | 飴、チョコレート、ゼリー飲料などがお勧め。但し、教室内では飲食できないので要注意！ |
| □ | 着席したら気になることがないか確認（机イスのがたつき、音響など） | 気になったらすぐに試験官に伝えよう。別の席に変えるなど対応してくれる。 |
| □ | 試験の最後の１～２分は、マークシートを「まとめて塗る」時間を確保 | 時間が足りず全問解けない場合、解き残しはまとめて適当にマークしよう。 |